THE PREPPER'S GUIDE TO FORAGING

How Wild Plants Can Supplement
a Sustainable Lifestyle

David Nash

Foreword by Todd Walker

SKYHORSE PUBLISHING

Skyhorse Publishing books may be purchased in bulk at special discounts for sales promotion, corporate gifts, fund-raising, or educational purposes. Special editions can also be created to specifications. For details, contact the Special Sales Department, Skyhorse Publishing, 307 West 36th Street, 11th Floor, New York, NY 10018 or info@skyhorsepublishing.com.

Skyhorse® and Skyhorse Publishing® are registered trademarks of Skyhorse Publishing, Inc.®, a Delaware corporation.

Visit our website at www.skyhorsepublishing.com.

10 9 8 7 6 5 4 3 2 1

Library of Congress Cataloging-in-Publication Data is available on file.

Cover design by Tom Lau
Cover images courtesy of iStock.com
All photos in insert courtesy of iStock.com
Illustrations by Sarah E. Cole

Print ISBN: 978-1-63450-493-5
Ebook ISBN: 978-1-63450-842-1

Printed in the United States of America

Table of Contents

To my friend W. Smith,
Thanks for all the help and support, but mostly all of the well deserved,
"That's a stupid idea, Dave"—because you still helped anyway.

Foreword

When David Nash asked me to write a foreword to his book, I was extremely honored and excited. I'm a student who enjoys doing common-sense stuff to become more self-reliant.

I like the fact that he's actually doing the stuff in his books, as well as the no-nonsense style of his writing based in humility. His attitude is always that of a student, whether teaching about guns or plants.

Knowledge is not enough to get you and your family through hard times when fragile systems fail. As much as we'd all like to think that food trucks will always deliver, a small glitch (or a dusting of snow in Georgia) is all it takes for the industrial food machine to grind to a halt. Not a problem. You've got food put aside for such occasions . . . if the trucks start rolling again soon.

What if they don't? I've read many misguided people who plan to "live off the land" in the backwoods. That's not what this book is about. David puts that myth to rest right up front. Foraging from the landscape is a skill meant to supplement your overall food independence plan. But what many foraging books don't give you is alternative uses for wild plants . . . and trees are rarely mentioned. Trees, my friend, are a four-season meal plan!

The more I learn about the natural world, the more I realize just how little I know. There are hundreds of thousands of plant species in nature. In my pursuit of outdoor self-reliance skills, knowledge of the plant world is the foundation of becoming less dependent on others. I'm not a botanist, but I do study plants and trees for their use as food and medicine. However, one of the best value-added aspects of this book has to be the alternative uses of each of the twenty-five plants listed. That alone is worth the price.

David also provides some excellent resources to further your journey in wildcrafting. The common sense advice to seek out a reputable plant forager is wise. Even then, you'll need to spend time in the woods or backyard practicing.

I would recommend locating and properly identifying two of the plants/trees each month. In one year's time, you'll have learned twenty-five plants and their uses. That would be a huge leap in your journey to self-reliance!

Todd Walker

Todd Walker, aka The Survival Sherpa, is an experienced survivalist who runs several websites and Facebook groups dedicated to wilderness survival and bushcraft.

Introduction

I spent a good portion of my childhood roaming the woods imagining I was a Native American, a mountain man, or a fugitive from justice (on the A-Team). As I explored I read every book on wilderness survival and edible plants I could find, but I also experimented by eating May apples, wild onions, and a variety of other wild edible plants. I was lucky because my father was a park ranger and I had access to experts and information that the typical kid did not. My views on wild edibles and sustainability were skewed toward my experiences (aren't everyone's?). As a result, I believed that "bugging out" to the wilderness during a disaster was a viable strategy.

As I matured, I began to realize how little wild land is actually available and how many people actually are on the planet. Once I married and started a family, I learned firsthand how much food it takes to feed even a small family, so my views started to change. Looking at what it takes to produce food and how much food a family of preppers needs to store, I began to see that my "bug out to the wild" dream was an unrealistic one.

I finally realized that the best way to survive a long-term disaster scenario is to have a place to "bug in" and grow the majority of my own family's food. This is not to say that foraging is not useful. I find it to be a valuable, if not vital, tool to supplement what I produce as well as to provide tools, medicine, and even chemicals that are essential to long-term subsistence living.

The Prepper's Guide to Foraging is not meant to be a plant guide or an exhaustive reference. I simply do not have the space, time, or resources to create a manual to cover all the North American plants that are edible. My goal is to create a blueprint and idea guide to help you see what is possible when you are open to the idea that you can use wild plants to supplement a sustainable lifestyle, where the majority of your family's food needs are addressed through a comprehensive plan that involves food storage and some manner of food production.

This book is designed to show how useful wild plants are by giving a food and alternative usage for easily identified plants that are commonly found throughout North America. I chose plants that are commonly identified, are edible, and have additional uses besides satisfying a growling stomach.

You may notice that the focus of this book is on trees. I am not biased against smaller life forms. However, as I choose the plants contained in this work, I made several conscious decisions that led me to a work that contained many trees. I will share two of them. The first reason I chose to include trees is that many other books that deal solely with wild edibles focus on smaller plants and I wanted to share less common information. Another is that I believe that trees are both easier to identify and better suited to a lifestyle where wild food *supplements*, not replaces, home produced/stored foods.

I strongly believe that the library of every outdoorsman, prepper, and survivalist needs at least two (if not more) high quality plant identification guides, as well as good reference material for plant use and edibility.

To help the reader identify those resources, I have added a bibliography of books that have been useful in my search for safe plant usage. I could not have completed this book without the information contained in that bibliography as well as a large amount of information gleaned from the Internet.

Part I

How to Learn About Wild Edible and Medicinal Plants

There are several ways to learn about wild forage foods, but only two that I think are appropriate and safe.

The Best Way

If you have access to a local expert—and I mean a real expert, not someone who read a book or two and threw together a YouTube channel—then the absolute best way to learn about wild plants is to take the time to study them together. This process takes a long time, maybe even years, but you will learn the most in the safest way possible. Going out into the woods with someone who can show you a plant, explain its habitat, and tell you about its uses, dangers, and methods of harvest is without a doubt the best way to safely learn.

When you have an expert show you the plant, you can smell it, taste it, and, most importantly, identify it in its natural surroundings. To put it another way, I can easily identify a tool by looking at a picture or seeing it lying on a bench alone, but it is much harder to identify the same tool when it's jumbled in among a bunch of other tools.

To be successful in foraging, you need to know a plant well enough so that you can skillfully hunt for a plant you have a particular need for, as well as quickly identify a food opportunity when you stumble upon it in a time of need.

The Next Best Way

I understand that not everyone has the time, ability, or personality to find and interact with an expert. It is hard to find someone who has the knowledge and is willing to invest the time and energy to share it with you. If you don't have access to an expert mentor, the next best way to safely learn is to spend the time doing the appropriate amount of research.

Do not rely solely on the Internet for your information. While I appreciate the power of the Internet, I do not use it for primary research when it comes to wild edible and medicinal plants, because quality control is nonexistent and mistakes can be fatal. It is very easy to create a website and present information, but it is much harder to present accurate information. The wide variety of Internet posts on "Mountain Dew Glow Sticks" or "How to Heat a Room Using Flowerpots and Tea Lights" well attests that not everyone with a website cares about presenting factual information when they can get fast views. I recommend that the majority of the time you spend in researching wild food be done in a well-stocked library.

I have a list of useful books at the back of this one. However, just as with the Internet, don't limit yourself to a single plant identification guide either. The biggest problem I have with plant guides is that they just don't have a lot of pictures. If you are going to trust your life on the identification of a plant you found in a book, then do yourself a favor and cross reference those pictures multiple times. Ensure that you check, cross-reference, and double-check your information as well as vetting the credentials of the author.

Bad Ways to Learn—Easy Ways to Die

It is no secret that with some things I like to play fast and loose. Guesstimating and improvising are two of my favorite skills when trying to get things done in a hurry. However, with some things (guns, moving heavy objects with cables, and eating wild things that can kill me) I force myself to go slow and work the right way.

As mentioned above, trusting only one source is a bad way to go. I prefer to gather five or more informational resources and vet them together to consider the totality of the facts before trusting my life to a piece of information.

Another way to learn is to pick up a plant in the woods and try it without fully vetting it. Just because something looks like something you read about does not mean it is safe to eat. Many edible plants share characteristics with poisonous plants, which could lead to a painful experience up to and including death.

Playing fast and loose with wild plants—either for food or medical purposes—is very similar to Russian roulette. You can die the first time you make a mistake, or you may be able to make bad decisions a few times before you pay the price. Personally, I don't feel the risk is worth the reward when proper tools for identification are so easy to find.

For this book, I have chosen plants that are very readily identifiable and/ or have very few plants that are comparable in looks. For example, it is very hard to misidentify a staghorn sumac with its red cone of berries or a sassafras tree with its three distinct leaf patterns, but please do not trust this book alone before you go out to the woods to try *any* of the projects or recipes in this book or any other. Cross-reference what you see with more than one other trusted source to ensure you always have accurate information.

Universal Edibility Test

Many discussions of foraging and wilderness survival will involve a mention of the "Universal Edibility Test." This test is supposed to allow a person to determine if they can safely eat a wild plant, but I agree with the opinion of expert forager Green Deane, who is against the use of this test. Many plants are extremely toxic, and consuming even a small amount will result in death. There are common plants that are so poisonous that you can take a bite of them in a hospital emergency department and die before you can be treated.

Upon studying the issue, I can't think of a situation where this test is worth it. In a wilderness survival situation that may come about by being lost in the woods, you are likely to be found before starvation occurs. In a long-term catastrophic disaster, you should have time to research the plants before you eat them.

Unless you desire death, and do not mind the possibility of an extremely painful end, do not eat any wild plant foraged unless you are 100 percent certain of the plant identification.

Personally, while I find plant identification guides to be a vital part of my prepper library, I take the additional step of getting identification of unknown plants from a local expert if I have *any* doubt about what I am looking at.

Some may take issue with the statement above, and rebut that the US Army includes the test in their survival manual. While this is true, I also know that the US military plays by averages and is not squeamish about losing a soldier or two in the attempt to save more.

With the above statements in mind, the most widely disseminated version of the edibility test is below:

Universal* Edibility Test

1. Do not eat for eight hours before performing the test so as not to involve food interactions.
   a. While fasting, test for contact poisoning by placing the plant inside your elbow or wrist for fifteen minutes to test for a reaction.
2. Wash the plant.
3. Test only one part of the plant at a time.
4. Separate the plant into components—in some cases one part of the plant may be edible while another is toxic.
5. Smell the component for strong or acidic odors (smell alone does not indicate a plant is edible or inedible).
6. Place a small portion of the plant component on your lip to test for burning or itching.
7. Wait three minutes after touching your lip. If you have not had a reaction during the three minutes, place a piece on your tongue.
8. Hold the food on your tongue for fifteen minutes.
9. If you have no reaction, chew and hold in your mouth for additional fifteen minutes.
   a. DO NOT swallow.
10. If you have not experienced any burning, itching, numbing, or other irritation after holding the chewed plant in your mouth for fifteen minutes, swallow it.
11. Wait eight hours without eating or drinking anything other than purified water.
12. If you have no ill effects during the eight-hour waiting period, eat ¼ cup of the prepared plant component.
13. Wait another eight hours, taking nothing but water. IF you have no ill effects, then the plant component tested may be considered safe.

I would love to have both a section on the common characteristics of edible plants and some signs a plant may be toxic, as there is a common list of plant

---

*Universal is a strong term, as this does not work universally.

signs to avoid. However, these signs can be misleading, and a quick statement that all aggregate berries growing in North America are safe to eat is false (even if it is a commonly held belief). For example, Goldenseal has an aggregate berry and grows in North America but is *not* edible.

While it is not possible to give a list of common characteristics of safe foods, here is a list of plant characteristics to avoid.

Do not eat plants that have:

- Milky or discolored sap.
- Beans, bulbs, or seeds inside pods.
- Bitter or soapy taste.
- Spines, fine hairs, or thorns.
- Dill, carrot, parsnip, or parsley-like foliage.
- Almond scent in woody parts and leaves.
- Grain heads with pink, purplish, or black spurs.
- Three-leaved growth pattern.

While this is a good start, this list is also full of misinformation as several of the plants in Part II have milky sap, taste bitter, or have fine hairs. No general list will keep you safe; you should rely on specific knowledge gained from reputable sources.

With approximately 90 percent of wild plants in North America being inedible, it pays to be very careful with what you put in your mouth.

Is Foraging an Appropriate Prepper Plan?

Like all prepper questions, the answer to this is a frustrating "It depends."

While some die-hard mountain men (and mountain men wannabes) will argue the point, there is simply not enough land to support the hunter-gatherer lifestyle.

In the book *The Economics of Subsistence Agriculture,* authors Colin Clark and M. R. Haswell claim that it takes approximately ninety-eight acres of ideal land to support a human being at the subsistence level. This is just one study, but it is on the conservative side of the issue* as estimates vary that 10 to 700 square miles of land are needed to support a single person.

We only have 3,805,927 square miles of land in America (including the extremely large portions of the country that are unavailable for foraging). In 2015, the US Census reported 321,216,397 people living in the country. You can easily understand that we simply do not have enough land for any attempt at a societal hunter-gather lifestyle. My math shows that each American would have a 7.5 acre parcel using the numbers above. I'll take the little section near the front gate of Fort Knox, but if I can't have the acreage containing that weird-looking cement building, I'll settle for some in Central Park. No matter

---

*98 acres is 0.15 square miles

the value of the land, 7.5 acres a person is not enough to feed the population using any type of hunter/gatherer lifestyle.

During the Great Depression, deer and turkey were hunted almost to extinction in large parts of America. Even with the scientific management of the deer population, enormous advances in hunting technology, and fewer hunters, many people that head to the woods to hunt are unable to harvest a deer. Imagine what it would be like to hunt in a forest full of hunters desperate to feed their family.

The math is clear that there is not enough land to use foraging as a means to gain food on a nationwide level, and even if there was, not everyone has the ability or opportunity to forage as a main source of food.

However, there are people in this country who have the knowledge, skill, and access required to find wild food to eat, but they are generally wise enough to not rely on foraging as a sole means of food gathering.

If you have the ability to do so, foraging for wild food and raw materials is a highly advantageous means to supplement stored items.

Foraging is a highly valuable skill, as all plants have some use. The ability to identify and apply those uses can come in handy when the neighborhood big box store is closed.

I am familiar with the dominant plants on my land and what uses I can get out of them. Having the knowledge of the plants in my area is vital to being able to supplement what I grow, buy, and store.

Knowing what I need and what I don't have allows me to seek out seeds so that I can plant perennials as a sort of food forest. The use of wise conservation and the introduction of appropriate wild plants into my property allow me to have what I need without having to spend a lot of energy in cultivation while still creating a sustainable supply chain that is just outside my front door.

Medicinal Uses
of Plants

Everything I have written on the benefits of foraging applies doubly so when it comes to the medicinal use of plants. Plants that may hurt or injure a healthy person can disable or kill someone that is ill. Some medicines work because they are toxic; however, too much of a good thing is probably not better in the case of medicine.

Every person is different, so too is every plant different. Wild ginseng that has to fight other plants for limited sun, water, and space is much stronger than cultivated ginseng grown under artificial shade. The same species of plant can have varying amounts and strengths of medicinal properties depending on where it was grown and when it was harvested.

There is a lot of misinformation from untrustworthy sources that present incomplete facts to those seeking information on foraging. Without getting into politics and attempting to stay neutral, the methods by which the Federal Food and Drug Administration test and approve new medicines make it virtually impossible for herbal remedies to be tested and marketed. No business entity can afford to spend hundreds of millions of dollars in testing plants (especially with living plants having such a variable nature) for medicinal properties, efficacy, and safety when they have no means of protecting their investment.

Without the federal stamp of approval, herbal medicine cannot be marketed as medicine, and practitioners cannot advertise or make specific claims that "X plant treats Y illness."

In this book, I am simply sharing what my experience has shown me. The plants and what they do from a medicinal standpoint are things that have worked for me, have worked for people I know personally, or are simply mentions of historical uses that may or may not work.

I am not a doctor and do not claim to be one. My medical training stops at the first responder level and I am not qualified to diagnose or treat illness. The common legal disclaimer of "speak with your doctor before trying anything found herein" applies. However, due to the following factors, many doctors either cannot or will not assist their patients in treating illness using herbal methods. Traditional medicine is generally prejudiced against herbal medicine.

Doctors are legally and ethically bound in how they treat illness. There is a lack of FDA-approved testing of herbal treatments. Additionally, there is a scarcity of accepted research of herbal medicine in peer reviewed medical journals. If you have a doctor who is knowledgeable in nontraditional medicine, is willing to work with you in finding treatments that are not based on commercial pharmaceuticals, and whom you trust, you have a valuable and rare resource.

Likewise, good medicinal books are also rare. I have researched, read, and reviewed many books that offer "home remedies" and find that most are either poorly documented, are based upon historical remedies that did not/do not work, or are copied from other works without any attempt to verify or explain the original content.

One book I feel very confident recommending, and one that I use extensively for knowledge on compounding the various remedies, is James Green's *The Herbal Medicine-Maker's Handbook: A Home Manual*. More than just a listing of "this plant treats this illness," Green's book tells how to transform raw plant into tinctures, compounds, teas, and elixirs and explains the benefits and pitfalls of the different treatment methods.

While still recommending additional research, the next few pages will explain some traditional parts of plants used for creating herbal medicines as well as the basic methods of using and producing herbal remedies.

Commonly Used Plant Parts

The individual parts of a plant have different properties and different uses. The root of a plant may be deadly poison, while the flower may have therapeutic properties.

How and when you harvest is also important. As I sit at my computer writing this book, I have a set of gourds drying on a rack in my kitchen that were harvested over a two-day period—the first are drying perfectly, while those harvested on the second day are fighting mold growth.

While there may be specific plants that require different processing, here are some basic instructions:

Guidelines for Harvesting and Storage

- Harvest plants on a dry day.
- Harvest sustainably; do not take all of the best specimens of the plant species in an area.
- Keep harvested materials out of direct sunlight.
- Dry them or use them quickly to reduce oxidation.
- Do not store plant materials if they are damp or they will mold.
- Take caution with plants growing near homes and occupied buildings or along roadsides as they may have been sprayed with pesticides.
- Plants growing in contaminated water or in water containing Giardia lamblia and other parasites are contaminated themselves.

- Individual edible plants may contain toxic compounds because of genetic or environmental factors. One example of this is the foliage of the common chokecherry. Some chokecherry plants have high concentrations of deadly cyanide compounds while others have low concentrations or none.
- Many valuable wild plants have high concentrations of oxalate compounds, also known as oxalic acid. Oxalates produce a sharp, burning sensation in your mouth and throat and damage the kidneys. Baking, roasting, or drying usually destroys these oxalate crystals. An example of this is the Indian turnip bulb, which you can eat only after removing these crystals by slow baking or by drying.

Common Plant Parts Used

Flowers:

Flowers are best harvested when fully open and after the morning dew has evaporated. Flowers damage easily, so be gentle. Cut the stem and harvest the flower whole.

If the flowers are tiny, treat them like they are seeds; if the flower is large or very fleshy, pick the individual petals and dry separately.

Leaves:

Harvest and dry large leaves individually. Small leaves (like mint leaves) are best harvested and dried on the stem in bunches.

Seeds:

I like to harvest a plant's entire seed head along with six inches or so of stalk. If you can catch the seeds just before they are totally ripe, you will prevent losing seed to birds or the wind.

If you hang the seed head over a paper bag, the seeds will fall into the bag as they dry. Sometimes, like with sunflowers, I will leave the flower on the plant and tie a paper bag around the still-growing flower. Then, once the seed is ready, I can harvest the seeds in the bag, which saves work.

Roots:

Most (but not all) roots should be harvested in the fall when the above-ground plant has withered. Winter temperatures make digging difficult, so do not wait too long.

Do not use too much water when cleaning, and do not wait too long to dry the root as some roots will absorb moisture and might become soft and begin to mold.

Wash the dirt off of the root and chop large roots into small pieces while green, as hard, dry roots can be very difficult to chop. I have shot bits of root around the kitchen while trying to chop too hard of a root.

Sap and Resin:

While the terms *sap* and *resin* are sometimes used interchangeably, they are two different things.

Sap is the plant's food and water. It is carried in the inner bark in the xylem and phloem cells and is comprised of sugar and water as well as minerals, hormones, and other nutrients. Tree sap is sometimes drinkable and can be reduced to syrup. Later in the book, I will discuss how to harvest sycamore sap to drink, ferment, or make delicious sycamore syrup.

Resin is much thicker than sap and is found in the outer tree bark layers. When a piece of tree bark is cut, resin is released to close the broken area, preventing the tree from getting infected. We will show how to use pine resin to make glue as well as a very bright torch.

You can harvest both sap and resin in the fall when the sap is falling by either making a deep incision or drilling a hole and attaching a cup to collect it.

Fruit:

Harvest berries and other fruits before they are overripe. Discard any fruit with signs of mold. Damaged fruits can still be used in most circumstances.

Bark:

Bark should be harvested in fall to minimize damage to the tree. Never gird the tree by removing bark in a ring completely around the tree. Girding will kill the tree. When American pioneers began farming a new plot of land in a forest, they would begin by girding trees to kill them so they could plant without the shade. In later years, the trees would be cut down.

Wipe down bark to remove moss, dirt, and insects. To dry, break bark into small pieces and dry on trays.

Bulbs:

You should generally harvest bulbs after the above-ground leaves have wilted and turned brown. However, with plants like garlic, this will cause you to harvest loose bulbs that will not store well. Some bulbs need to be harvested when the leaves are still green. Either way, do not pull the bulb up by the leaves, but rather loosen the ground away from the root to allow the bulb to be harvested gently. Wash, but do not use more water than necessary. Dry thoroughly without breaking the bulb. One thing to consider when harvesting the bulbs of plants is that you will kill the plant. This means is it vitally necessary to take no more than one quarter to one third of the plants in a stand. When you are gathering bulbs for food, and the bulbs are small, consider a more sustainable food source, as it will not take long to decimate a population of plants in an area.

Basic Types of Herbal Treatments

There are several standard types of treatments that are common to herbal medicine. While specific procedures may change for a particular plant, patient, or use, the types of remedies listed below are standard to the art.

Note that if you mix plants, then the total amount of material should not exceed the recommended quantity. For example, if a recipe requires three teaspoons of herb to one cup of water and you want to mix dandelion, willow bark, and sassafras, then use one teaspoon of each.

While not every method is used in this book, I felt it necessary to include them in the event your research mentions a type we did not cover in the later projects and recipes.

Infusion:

An infusion is the simplest way to use medicinal plants. It is basically making a tea. Infusions are made with hot but not quite boiling water. The steam released by boiling can disperse volatile oils in the plants. Infusions are often used with flowers and leafy parts of the plant.

Standard Infusion Recipe:

Material:

- 1 ounce dried herbs or 2½ ounces fresh plant material
- 2 cups water

Procedure:

- Put plant material in pot with tight-fitting lid.
- Bring water to a boil.
- Remove water from stove and pour over plant.
- Let steep for 10 minutes.
- Strain through fine sieve.

This makes three doses.

Decoction:

This is a more involved process than an infusion, but it extracts much more of the plant's active ingredients. It is used for tougher plant materials such as roots, bark, twigs, and berries.

Standard Decoction Recipe:

Material:

- 1 ounce dried herbs or 2 ounces fresh plant material
- 3 cups water

Procedure:

- Put plant material in saucepan.
- Add cold water and bring to a boil.
- Simmer for 1 hour or until volume has been reduced to 2 cups.
- Strain through fine sieve.

This makes three doses.

Tincture:

Steeping the plant material in alcohol makes a tincture. Tinctures are appropriate to any part of a plant. Not only does the alcohol in a tincture act as a solvent to extract the plant's active ingredients, but it also acts as a preservative. Unlike infusions and decoctions that need to be made fresh daily, a tincture can be made in advance and stored. Tinctures should be made with single plants, although tinctures can be combined once made. Vodka or pure grain alcohol is ideal for making tinctures because they contain few additives, but rum or whiskey may disguise the taste of herbs that are not palatable.

Standard Tincture Recipe:

Material:

- 7 ounces dried herbs or 1¼ pounds fresh plant material
- 1½ pints 80-proof vodka
- 1 ounce water

Procedure:

- Put plant material in large jar with tight-fitting lid. Mix water and alcohol.
- Pour liquid into jar and seal tightly.
- Shake the jar vigorously.
- Store in a cool, dry, dark place for 2 weeks, shaking the jar every day.
- Strain mixture through a cheesecloth and into a container.
- Squeeze out all liquid contained in the mixture.
- Pour captured tincture into a dark glass container, label well, and store sealed.

This makes approximately 150 teaspoon-sized doses.

Non-Alcoholic Tinctures:

Sometimes alcohol is not suitable for a patient, a pregnant woman, small child, or someone with liver issues. It is possible to evaporate the alcohol by adding an ounce and a half of almost-boiling water to a teaspoon dose of a tincture and allowing it to cool.

Syrup:

Honey or other unrefined sugar is used to preserve an infusion or decoction. Syrups are often used as a cough remedy. The sweetness of the syrup can mask bad-tasting remedies, so they are often used with children.

Standard Syrup Recipe:

Material:

- 1 pint infusion or decoction
- 1 pound honey or unrefined sugar

Procedure:

- Heat infusion or decoction in a saucepan.
- Add honey or sugar.
- Stir constantly until dissolved.
- Allow mixture to cool.
- Pour into a dark glass container.

Seal with a cork, as syrups can ferment and cause a screw-top jar to explode (action slows in the refrigerator).

This makes approximately 200 teaspoon-sized doses.

Infused Oils:

Not all ingredients are water or alcohol soluble and need to be extracted in oil. Infused oils are particularly good for making massage oils, creams, and ointments. There are two methods listed below for making infused oils: the hot and cold methods. Infused oils store well and can last up to a year if stored in a cool, dry, dark place.

Hot Infusion:

Some plants extract better using hot oil, comfrey being one of them.

Standard Hot Oil Infusion Recipe:

Material:

- 9 ounces dried herbs or 1½ pounds fresh plant material
- ½ quart oil (sunflower, extra virgin olive oil, grape seed, or peanut oil)

Procedure:

- Put plant material and oil in a glass bowl in a heavy pot (or use a double boiler). Alternatively, you can put a glass bowl in a crock-pot.
- Heat gently for 3 hours.
- Pour mixture into cheesecloth and let drain into a container.
- Store in an airtight glass bottle with an airtight lid.

Cold Infusion:

Some active ingredients in plant medicinals break down by heat and need a gentler method of extraction. This works best with flowers.

Standard Cold Oil Infusion Recipe:

Material:

- Twice as many flowers to pack tightly into a quart mason jar
- 1 quart oil (Cold-pressed oil is best, but you can use walnut oil or any of the oils listed in the hot oil infusion recipe.)

Procedure:

- Pack jar tightly with plant material.
- Fill jar with oil.
- Tightly screw on lid and place jar on a sunny windowsill.
- Let steep 3 weeks.
- Strain through cheesecloth.
- Refill jar with fresh flowers, discarding the previously oil-soaked flower heads.
- Refill with once-steeped oil.
- Repeat steeping and draining steps.
- Drain into dark glass jar.

Cream:

A cream is a mixture of water with fats. The emulsion of water and oils allows the treatment to be absorbed into the skin. Homemade creams can last for several months, but cold storage in the refrigerator will extend the storage life. This method is appropriate for most plants.

Standard Cream Recipe:

Material:

- 3 ounces dried plant material
- 2 ounces Lanette wax (or emulsifying ointment BP)
- 2 cups water
- ⅕ tablespoon glycerin

Procedure:

- Melt Lanette wax in a double boiler.
- Gently mix in water to make base emulsifying cream.
- Add herbs and glycerin.

- Mix.
- Heat gently for 3 hours.
- Strain through sieve.
- Stir constantly until cool.
- Spoon into jar with a spatula. Small jelly jars work best. It is easier to scrape the spatula on the edges to fill first and then fill the center.

Ointment:

An ointment does not have water in it, so it does not absorb into the skin. It is best used when the skin is broken, weak, or in need of protection. Diaper rash cream and zinc sunburn cream are ointments. Historically, ointments were made with animal fat like rendered lard, but petroleum jelly or paraffin wax is appropriate.

Standard Ointment Recipe:

Material:

- 2 ounces dried plant material
- 1 pound petroleum jelly or soft paraffin wax

Procedure:

- Melt jelly or wax in a double boiler.
- Stir in herbs.
- Add herbs and glycerin.
- Heat gently for 2 hours.
- Strain through sieve.
- Stir constantly until cool.
- Spoon into jar with a spatula. Small jelly jars work best. It is easier to scrape the spatula on the edges to fill first and then fill the center.

Powders:

Dried herbs can be powdered and later stirred into liquids, taken as capsules, sprinkled over food, and taken directly. Dried herbs can be powdered using a mortar and pestle starting in the center of the mortar and turning the pestle in gradually larger circles until the material is ground to a powder. Alternatively, you can use a blender.

Empty gelatin capsules can be purchased rather cheaply on the Internet, and you can fill the capsules by hand with a small scoop or by sliding the two capsule ends together through a bowl of the powdered herb. However, I think just buying a capsule filler tray is easier and more time efficient.

Compress:

A compress is a cloth pad soaked in a tincture, decoction, or infusion and placed on an injured area of the body. This is most typically used for headaches, but it has been used for strains and sprains. I have heard of a willow bark tea being used as a compress externally on headaches, but I do not have personal experience with it.

Standard Compress Recipe:

Material:

- Standard infusion, decoction, or 4 teaspoons tincture mixed with 2 cups of hot water
- Cloth pad made of cotton or linen (alternatively you could use cotton balls and surgical gauze)

Procedure:

- Gently warm liquid.
- Soak cloth in warm medicinal liquid.
- Wring out excess liquid from cloth.
- Hold pad over the injured area.
- When the pad cools or dries out, reapply warm liquid and replace over injured area.

Poultice:

A poultice is similar to a compress, but instead of an extract, the plant or paste made from the material is placed over the injury and held in place by the cloth. While poultices are generally applied hot, cold fresh leaves are often just as suitable. Dried and powdered herbs can be mixed with water to make a paste and used on a poultice also.

Standard Poultice Recipe:

Material:

- Enough fresh plant or plant paste to cover injured area.
- Cloth pad made of cotton or linen (alternatively you could use cotton balls and surgical gauze)
- 1 teaspoon oil

Procedure:

- Boil fresh plant material.
- Spread a little oil over injured area to prevent herb from sticking.
- Squeeze out surplus liquid and spread plant on affected area.
- Apply cloth pad over the injured area and tie loosely to keep herbal treatment in place.

Steam Inhalants:

Some medicinal plants are best inhaled by placing them in a bowl of boiling water and inhaling the steam. This works well for dealing with mucus, asthma, or sinusitis.

Standard Procedure for Steam Inhalants:

Material:

- 2 tablespoons dried herb
- 1 pint boiling water

Procedure:

- Add treatment to a bowl and pour boiling water over it.
- Lean your head over the bowl.
- Cover head and bowl with large towel.
- Inhale deeply for as long as you can stand the heat or until mixture cools.
- Do not go to a cold environment for at least half an hour after steam treatment.

Tonic Wines:

Ginseng and some other roots are sometimes infused into wine. Bitter herbs infused as wines (known as bitters) have been used as after-dinner drinks for hundreds of years. Wine can make herbal remedies more tolerable, are easier on the body than tinctures made with harder spirits, and are generally a great way to consume herbal remedies. Herbal wines last about one year.

Standard Tonic Wine Recipe:

Material:

- 1 ounce dried herb
- 1 pint wine (Generally a sweeter wine with about 12 percent alcohol is better.)

Procedure:

- Fill bottle with herbs.
- Pour wine over herbs to fill the bottle.
- Cap tightly and shake well.
- Store in a cool, dark place, shaking every day for 2 weeks.
- Strain herbs.
- Some liqueurs need maturation time, in which case you should wait a month or more.

Botanical Description Definitions

While I took care not to get too technical in my descriptions of the common plants used in Part II of this book, you will need to have a working knowledge of the terminology if you want to be effective in researching wild plants.

It is very hard to accurately describe plants without the ability to understand basic botanical definitions.

Knowing the correct terms will also identify you as someone who cares about the subject, which is vital in gaining the support of your local expert. I used to teach radiological response, and I taught the same basic class to cops, volunteer firemen, foresters, nurses, and doctors. When describing the symptoms of acute radiation sickness to laymen, I could get away with saying something like, "If you vomit within an hour of exposure, you're probably going to die," but if I said the same thing (it did not matter if the statement was accurate) to a doctor, he or she would immediately label me as a novice or someone without knowledge. It would be different if I used the more technically accurate "Emesis within one hour of acute exposure is a positive sign that a lethal dose of radiation was received." It is the same with botany as it is in any other professional field: correct terms are more accurate and will yield a better result when talking among those in the field.

Here are some common terms organized into groups based upon stem, leaf, and flowers.

Stem Parts:

The term *stem* refers to the structure that provides support to the plant. It acts as both the skeleton and the circulatory system and connects the roots to the leaves and flowers. There can be either a single stem originating from the roots with lateral stems growing from it, many different stems coming out from the roots, or a combination of the two. Where there is just one stem coming from the roots of a woody perennial (tree), it is known as a "trunk."

Branch/lateral growth/side shoot: These different terms are used to describe stems that come out of the main stem. In general, they are slightly slimmer than the main stem or trunk of the plant.

Node: The node is the part of a plant stem from which one or more leaves emerge. Nodes often form a slight swelling or knob.

Internode: An internode is the area of a stem between two nodes.

Bud: A bud is an undeveloped or embryonic shoot. Buds most often occur at the tip of the stem or at the connection between leaf and stem.

Stipule: Stipules are small leaf-like appendages to a leaf, which are typically found in pairs at the base of the leaf stalk. Stipules come in a variety of forms, but not every plant has stipules.

Leaf Parts

Leaves grow out of nodes and are the organ of a plant that produces food. Oxygen and moisture is released from the leaf.

Axil: The axil is the connection between the leaf or leaf stem (petiole) and the stem or branch that supports the leaf.

Blade: The broad thin part of a leaf apart from the stalk is called the leaf blade (this may often be called a "lamina").

Petiole: A petiole is the stalk-like portion of a plant that joins a leaf to a stem. It is generally flexible so the leaf can move in the wind, and some petioles will turn to orientate the lead blade toward the sun.

Sessile: Sessile is a term that describes a leaf that grows directly out of a stem without the benefit of a petiole.

Stipules: The stipules are two small flaps that grow at the base of the petiole of some plants. Some stipules, such as those of willows and certain cherry trees, produce substances that prevent insects from attacking the developing leaf.

Leaf Types

Leaves take on many shapes and are a vital part of plant identification. Most plant identification guides use these terms so that positive identification can be made:

Simple: Simple leaves are not divided or branched. Oaks, maples, and most deciduous tress have simple leaves of one leaf blade attached to a single petiole.

Compound: Compound leaves consist of two or more simple parts or individuals in combination. The blades of a compound leaf are fully subdivided into leaflets. A clover is an example of compound leaf, as is the black walnut.

Leaf Arrangements

Different terms are usually used to describe the arrangement of leaves on the stem:

Alternate: The leaves are placed alternately on the two sides of the stem. There will be only one leaf per node.

Opposite: In an opposite arrangement, there are two leaves per node. The leaves grow in opposed pairs, one on each side of the stem.

Whorled: A whorled arrangement is a set of leaves, flowers, or branches springing from the stem at the same level and encircling it. There are three or more leaves per node.

Spiral: In a spiral arrangement, there is one leaf per node, and it will generally corkscrew around the stem.

Flower Parts

Flowers are responsible for plant reproduction. This is where the seed, nut, berry, or drupe is formed. Flowers are very distinctive, and when present, greatly assist in positive plant identification.

Pedicel/peduncle: This is the stalk that supports the flower. Where this is a solitary flower it is called a peduncle. Where there is a grouping of flowers, each flower is attached to a stalk called a pedicel. Pedicels are then attached to a peduncle, which attaches the group of flowers and pedicels to the plant.

Receptacle: The receptacle supports all parts of the flower and attaches them to the pedicel/peduncle.

Sepal: The sepals are small, petal-like structures that sit below the petals and often form the covering of the flower when it is in bud form. They are often green and relatively thick. Collectively, these form the calyx.

Petals: Petals are the larger, usually colorful structures, which surround the fertile parts of the flower. When the petals are brightly colored, it is usually to attract bees and other pollinators to the flower. Collectively, the petals form the corolla.

Tepal: Where the sepals and petals are fused into one structure it is called a tepal. In reality a tepaled flower just looks like petals without sepals below them. Tulips are a common example of a plant with tepals.

Anther: The anther is the organ that produces the pollen sacs that will release pollen to fertilize the female ovule.

Filament: The filament is the stalk that supports the anthers and holds them at the right height to maximize opportunities for pollination.

Ovary: The ovary is the female portion of the flower that contains the ovule.

Ovule: The ovule contains the egg cells that will be fertilized by the male pollen. The ovule eventually develops into a seed and the ovary into a fruit.

Style: The style is the long structure that reaches from the ovary to the stigma. The pollen landing on the stigma must travel through the style to reach the ovary.

Stigma: The stigma is covered with a sticky substance that the pollen sticks to and feeds from before traveling down the style to fertilize the egg cell in the ovule.

Types of Fruit

There are many different end results to plant fertilization. All are developed to ensure that seeds become new plants. Fruits are divided into either fleshy fruits or dry fruits.

Fleshy fruits are further subdivided by whether the fruit is formed by a single flower or a group of flowers. They can have one seed or several seeds.

Berry, drupe, aggregation of drupes, pome, and hesperidium are types of fleshy fruits formed from a single flower, while sorosis, syconium, and coenocarpium are formed from a group of flowers.

Dry fruits are divided by whether or not the seeds are contained in a seedpod of some sort, or not. Seeds with seedpods are classified as dehiscent, while those without are called indehiscent.

Dry dehiscent fruits are follicle, legume, silique, and capsule.

Dry indehiscent fruits are achene, nut, samara, caryopsis.

Knowing the type of fruit a plant has might help you to identify it and might also help you to know when the seeds are ready to harvest.

Berry: A single fleshy fruit without a stone, usually containing a number of seeds. Tomatoes are an example of a berry.

Drupe: A single fleshy fruit with a hard stone, which contains the single seed. A cherry or a peach is an example of a drupe.

Aggregation of Drupes: A fleshy fruit, made up of many drupes but formed from a single flower, each drupe containing one seed. A blackberry is an example of this.

Pome: A fleshy fruit with a thin skin that is not formed from the ovary. The seeds are contained in chambers in the center of the fruit. Apples are pomes.

Hesperidium: A berry with a tough, aromatic rind. Oranges, lemons, and limes are good examples of hesperidiums.

Pseudocarp: A pseudocarp is a false fruit, because it does not contain the seeds. The seeds are achenes, on the outside of a fleshy fruit. Strawberries are the best example of pseudocarps.

Follicle: A dry dehiscent fruit that splits on one side only. It may contain one or many seeds. The milkweed described in Part II is an example of a follicle.

Legume: A dry dehiscent pod that splits on two sides. Peas and peanuts are commonly known legumes.

Silique: A dry dehiscent fruit that is long and thin, splits down the two long sides, and has a papery membrane (the septum) between the two halves. Cabbages and radishes are both silique seeds.

A silique that is less than twice as long and broad is called a **silicula**.

Capsule: A dry fruit which splits open to release the seeds. It is the most common fruit type. Cotton, horse Chestnut, jimson weed, and witch hazel are all well-known examples of capsules.

Achene: A single-seeded dry indehiscent fruit in which the seed coat is not part of the fruit coat. A sunflower has achene seeds.

Nut: A large, single, hardened achene. Chestnuts, acorns, hickory, and walnuts are all common nuts.

Caryopsis: A simple dry indehiscent fruit, like an achene, but with the seed coat fused with the fruit coat. Many caryopsis have been domesticated for food usage—corn, oats, rice, rye, and wheat are all examples of this.

Samara: An independent, dry indehiscent fruit that has part of the fruit wall extended to form a wing. Maples are examples of this type of seed.

Part II

A listing of twenty-five common plants, their illustrated descriptions, their range of habitat, and a description of at least one food and alternative use.

American Basswood

Basswood leaf and flower

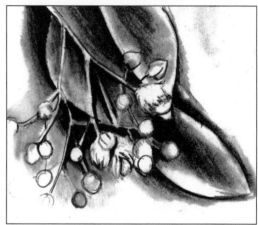
Basswood seed pod

Scientific Name: *Tilia Americana*

Type of Plant: Tree

Description: American basswood is a deciduous tree that grows 60 to 130 feet tall and three to four feet in diameter. This tree grows faster than most other American hardwoods. The bark of the American basswood is gray to light brown, with narrow and well-defined fissures. Twigs of this tree are smooth and reddish green. Second-year twigs are light gray, turning dark brown or brownish gray in later years. The twigs are marked with dark, wart-like growths. The leaves are long and broad with unequal bases (but the side nearest the branch is larger) and are alternately arranged, asymmetrical, coarsely serrated, and four to eight inches (though they can grow up to ten inches). Fully-grown leaves are dark green in color and smooth, with shiny tops and pale undersides. The leaves have tufts of brown hairs and are paler beneath with tufts of rusty brown hairs in the points of divergence of the primary veins. The twigs and leaves both contain mucilaginous sap.

Natural Range: American basswood ranges from Canada to North Carolina, westward through Tennessee, and into Arkansas, the Dakotas, Nebraska, Kansas, and Northeast Oklahoma.

Food Usage: Both the leaves and flowers are both edible, but the young leaves are tender and the best to eat. Bees pollinate the American basswood and create a popular light honey from its nectar. If you ever find basswood (also known as linden) honey, you may want to try it. Linden honey has a pleasing aftertaste that goes very well with breakfast teas such as Earl Grey.

Basswood Salad:

In spring and early summer, basswood leaves make a good salad green. The leaves have the sweetest flavor and tenderness when the buds have just opened. However, for several weeks into the growing season, the youngest leaves at the tips of new growth are suitable for eating.

When the leaves are tough, they are too old for eating. You can also tell the youngest leaves because they are smaller, shinier, and lighter in color than more mature leaves.

Alternative Usage: American basswood has been used as a medicinal plant.

American basswood flowers are used to treat cold and flu symptoms as well as infections, hypertension, and headaches (especially migraines).

The flowers ingested as a tea act as a diuretic, an antispasmodic, and a sedative. Basswood flower tea also relieves anxiety-related indigestion, irregular heartbeat, and vomiting.

Basswood that has been converted to charcoal can be ingested in small amounts to treat intestinal disorders and can be used topically to treat edema or infection, such as cellulitis or ulcers of the lower leg.

Basswood Tea
Material:
- 6–10 basswood flowers
- Water

Procedure:

• Pour 1 cup of boiling water over 6 to 10 flowers.
• Steep for 5 minutes.

Drink 1 to 2 cups per day.

Warning: Do not use flower tea for an extended period as prolonged use may cause heart problems in some cases.

Note: The wood is soft with fine close grain; it is clear of knots but does not easily split. Basswood planes, glues, screws, and holds nails well. Because it is odorless, the wood is used in the manufacture of woodenware, cheap furniture, and bodies of carriages. It is also especially adapted for wood carving, but it should be noted that it rots easily.

The inner bark is very tough and fibrous, used in the past for making ropes.

Birch

Birch leaf

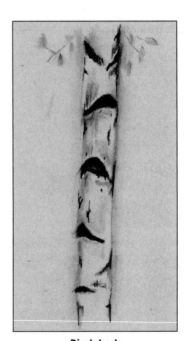

Birch bark

Scientific Name: *Betula*

Type of Plant: Tree

Description: Birch is a thin-leaved, deciduous hardwood tree that is closely related to the beech/oak family. It is typically a rather short-lived pioneer species widespread in the Northern Hemisphere.

The birch is a medium-sized tree, reaching 60 feet tall with a three-foot diameter trunk.

The bark is white and flakes off in horizontal strips, and the tree often has small black marks and scars.

In trees younger than five years, the bark appears brown, which makes it much harder to identify. The leaves are alternate, ovate, one to five inches long, and two to four inches broad, with a serrated edge.

Natural Range: The birch is found worldwide and across North America. The trees thrive in moist soil but require full sunlight. Birches prefer damp and cool environments. Because they have shallow root systems this root system makes them susceptible to drought.

Birches are often found in even-aged forest stands because they are a pioneer species and rapidly colonize open ground following a disturbance or fire.

Food Usage: The sap can be drunk similar to coconut water. Birch sap is easy to collect. Simply drill a hole into the trunk and lead the sap into a container with a tube or a thin twig; surface tension will cause the sap to follow the twin into a jar tied around the tree. Birch sap has to be collected in early spring before any green leaves have appeared, as waiting longer will yield a bitter sap.

Birch Sap Wine

Ingredients:

- 1 gallon birch sap (3–4 trees)
- 2½–3 pounds sugar
- 8 ounces chopped raisins (or wine nutrient)
- Peel and juice 1–2 lemons
- A general-purpose fermenting yeast (bread yeast can be used, but a high-alcohol yeast is best)

Procedure:

- Bring the tree sap to a boil then reduce the heat.
- Add the sugar and stir until dissolved.
- Simmer for 12 minutes and then remove from heat.
- Place the raisins in a suitable plastic fermenting bucket and pour in the liquid.
- Allow the liquid to cool.
- Add the lemon peel and juice.

- Add the yeast.
- Cover the bucket, leaving room for gas to escape, then leave to ferment for 5 days in a warm place.
- After 5 days, strain the liquid into a container and seal with an airlock.
- Leave to ferment, usually for 2 to 3 months.
- Pour into a clean container and allow the sediment to settle for 24 to 48 hours.
- Bottle the wine and leave for another 2 to 3 months before drinking.

Alternative Usage: Tar for natural glue. The use of birch-bark resin dates as far back as the Paleolithic era. More than just being used as a glue, it was used to seal boats and water containers, waterproofing for shelters, an antibacterial covering for wounds, a flammable fire source, and as a chewing gum.

Birch-bark resin is useful as it is solid at 65° Fahrenheit, but changes form as it heats.

- 85° Fahrenheit, it can be molded in your hands.
- 105° Fahrenheit, it acts as a putty.
- 135° Fahrenheit, birch bark tar is a softer, sticky putty.
- At 352° Fahrenheit, it boils.

Unlike pine pitch, birch bark-tar is not made from the sap of birch trees. Heating birch bark in an oven with little air is needed to extract the oil from birch bark. The birch-bark oil will sweat out of the bark and run to the bottom of your oven.

Birch-Bark Tar Collection:

Materials:

- 1 gallon paint can with lid
- Empty soup can
- Birch bark

Procedure:

- Punch a hole in the center of the bottom of the paint can.
- Trim birch bark so it is a little shorter than the paint can. Roll the bark together and insert in the can. When inserting the bark, be careful that you do not fill the can so full that you cover up the center hole.
- Place lid on can and close it tightly.

- Dig a hole deep enough so that you can insert your soup can. Your soup can should sit in the hole with the rim at ground level.
- Place your soup can in the hole, making sure that it is stable and level.
- Place the paint can over the soup can so that the hole in the bottom of the can sits over the center of the paint can. Make sure there are no air gaps between the two cans.
- Use dirt to create a seal around the two cans to keep them together and to ensure nothing falls into the soup can.
- Start a fire over and around the condensing can and keep it burning for an hour or so. The fire does not need to be large, but the paint can should glow a dull red.
- Once the fire has burned down and cooled, scrape the dirt away, once again being careful not to allow dirt to fall into the soup can.
- Your birch-bark tar will be in the soup can.
- To thicken the oil, slowly simmer it over a low heat for about an hour or so until it becomes quite gooey and is about half the original volume.

Note: Birch foliage is used as a food by the larvae of a large number of butterflies and moths.

Birch sawdust can be added to flour to extend it. The inner bark is edible and can be used as a flour substitute, but it will not rise.

The wood of birches catches fire even if wet.

Blackberries

Blackberry leaves

Blackberry fruit

Scientific Name: *Rubus fruticosus*

Type of Plant: Bramble

Description: The *bramble*, a word meaning any impenetrable thicket, has traditionally been applied specifically to the blackberry or its products.

They are the largest of all berries. They are plump and have a purple-black color. In reality, blackberries are not berries at all; they are tiny fruits clustered together around a core. Each tiny fruit contains a little seed.

Natural Range: Throughout the United States, Europe, and Asia

Food Usage: The berries have been enjoyed by multiple cultures throughout the ages.

Blackberry Sauce
Ingredients:

- 3½ cups fresh blackberries
- ¼ cup sugar or honey
- ¼ cup water
- 1 tablespoon lemon juice

Procedure:

- Bring blackberries, sugar, and water to a simmer in a medium saucepan, stirring occasionally.
- Simmer over low heat for 5 minutes.
- Strain through a fine sieve into a bowl.
- Stir in lemon juice.
- Cover and refrigerate until chilled.

Alternative Usage: Medicinal

Tannin-rich blackberries have long been used as folk treatments. Blackberry tea has been said to help treat diarrhea.

Blackberry Tea
Ingredients:

- Dried blackberry leaves
- 1½ cups water

Procedure:

- Boil 2 tablespoons of dried blackberry leaves in 1½ cups water for 10 minutes.
- Strain.
- Drink a cup several times a day.

Note: Blackberries are perennial plants that typically bear biennial stems from their root system.

Cattails

Cattail rush

Cattail flower spike

Scientific Name: *Typha latifolia*

Type of Plant: Perennial

Description: Cattail leaves are on a simple, jointless stem that bears the flowering spikes. The flowers form a narrow spike at the top of the vertical stem. The seeds are minute and attached to fine hairs. When ripe, the heads disintegrate into a cottony fluff from which the seeds are dispersed by wind.

Natural Range: Cattails are found in wetland habitats throughout the Northern Hemisphere.

Food Usage: Many parts of the plant are edible by humans. The starchy rhizomes are nutritious with protein content comparable to corn or rice. They are most often harvested from late autumn to early spring. The outer portion of young plants can be peeled, and the heart can be eaten raw or it can be boiled and eaten like asparagus.

Cattail on the Cob

Ingredients:

- 30–40 cattail flower heads, peeled
- Water
- Butter

Procedure:

- Boil cattail flower heads in water for 10 minutes.
- Drain the cattail flower heads and slather them generously with butter.
- Eat them just like miniature corn on the cob.

Alternative Usage: Some Native Americans used the seed hairs as tinder for starting fires. Some tribes also used cattail down to line moccasins and for bedding, diapers, baby powder, and cradleboards.

Cattails can be dipped in wax or fat and then lit as a candle, with the stem serving as a wick. Without the use of wax or fat, it will smolder slowly, somewhat like incense, and may repel insects.

Cattail Candle

Material:

- Dry cattail flower heads
- Rendered lard
- Stick with sharpened end

Procedure:

- Dip the cattail head into a container filled with melted lard, wax, or oil. The higher quality of fuel you use, the better your candle will perform.
- Remove the cattail and let the melted fat harden.
- Insert the stick into the head.
- Light the cattail. This candle is more of a torch and can burn upward of 6 hours, producing a lot of light and heat.

Note: No green plant produces more edible starch per acre than cattails. In addition, cattails can be used to produce shelter, fire, baskets, and much more.

Comfrey

Comfrey plant

Comfrey flower

Scientific Name: *Symphytum officinale L*

Type of Plant: Perennial

Description: Comfrey is a perennial herb with a black, turnip-like root and large, broad, and hairy leaves. Comfrey bears small bell-shaped flowers of various colors (but most often purple or cream). These flowers can also appear to be striped. It likes to grow in damp, grassy places and is often found on riverbanks and ditches. Because it is tolerant of many different soil conditions and can sow itself, comfrey can spread rapidly.

Natural Range: Comfrey is hardy from zones 4 to 9 and will grow in full or partial sun.

Food Usage: Comfrey leaves have a hairy and rough texture as the leaves age, making it unappetizing to eat. However, because it is a good source of vitamins and minerals such as magnesium and selenium, as well as being very high in Vitamin A, riboflavin, potassium, manganese, and dietary fiber, it is worth the trouble. Young leaves and buds are very tender.

Comfrey Dip
Ingredients:

- 1 cup comfrey leaves
- 1 cup natural yogurt
- 1 tablespoon good honey
- 1 squeeze lemon juice

Procedure:

- Mix together all ingredients in a blender.
- This makes a dip similar to tzatziki sauce.

Alternative Usage: Comfrey has been used as a medicinal herb for thousands of years. Its traditional names of knitbone and boneset attest to this. Comfrey was used to treat a wide variety of illness and injury such as:

- Bronchial problems
- Broken bones
- Sprains, arthritis
- Gastric and varicose ulcers
- Severe burns
- Acne and other skin conditions

Comfrey Healing Salve*
Materials:

- 2 cups comfrey leaf
- 2 cups olive oil
- ⅔ cup grated beeswax

Procedure:

- Put the comfrey leaf into a jar and pour in oil until the jar has just 1½ inches open space at the top.
- Tightly apply the lid and place the jar in a large pot on the stove.
- Fill the pot with water up to 2 inches from the top of the jar and turn the heat to low.
- Allow the comfrey to infuse into the oil for at least 12 but no more than 24 hours.
- Do not allow the water to simmer, and keep adding hot water as needed to maintain the water level.
- Once the oil is dark green, put grated beeswax into a medium saucepan.
- Pour the oil through the fine mesh strainer and over the beeswax.
- Turn the heat to low and whisk until all of the beeswax has melted.
- Pour the oil into your chosen containers and allow to cool for 24 hours.
- Keep the salve in a cool, dark place.

Note: In modern herbalism, comfrey is most commonly used topically. Some experts say that it should be restricted to topical use and should never be ingested, as it contains dangerous amounts of hepatotoxic pyrrolizidine alkaloids (PA) that damage the liver.

Due to the presence of PAs, many countries have laws restricting the distribution, sale, and/or use of comfrey. The PA content is greatest in the roots and is less in the leaves, with older leaves containing less than younger ones.

A liquid fertilizer can also be made from the comfrey plant by steeping chopped comfrey leaves in water for several weeks until they form a dark, thick liquid. The liquid should be diluted 12:1 before application.

A potting mixture can also be made from leaf mold derived from chopped comfrey leaves and dolomite mixed together and left to sit in a lidded container for several months. Though not suitable for seeds, once well rotted the comfrey leaf mixture is a good general potting soil.

---

*Do not use on dirty skin, as this promotes rapid healing of superficial wounds, and may cause skin to heal over bacteria.

Common Yarrow

Yarrow leaf

Yarrow flower

Scientific Name: *Achillea millefolium*

Type of Plant: Perennial

Description: Common yarrow is an erect, herbaceous, perennial plant that produces one to several stems approximately three feet in height. Leaves are evenly distributed along the stem, with the leaves near the middle and bottom of the stem being the largest. The leaves have varying degrees of hair. The leaves are two to eight inches long, feathery, and arranged spirally on the stems. The plant has a strong, sweet scent, similar to that of chrysanthemums.

Natural Range: Common yarrow prefers sunny locations on thin, sandy soils, although it can grow in partly sunny conditions as well. Yarrow is commonly found along roadsides, in fields, waste areas, and canyon bottoms, and even on lawns. It grows in North America, Europe, Asia, Australia, Africa, and South America.

Food Usage: Leaves can be consumed raw or cooked. They have a somewhat bitter flavor, yet they make a great addition to mixed salads. They are best used when young.

Common yarrow leaves are also used as a hop substitute to help flavoring and preserve for beer.

Yarrow Pasta

Ingredients:

- 8 ounces dried penne pasta
- 4 tablespoons fresh garlic, finely chopped
- Pinch of Kosher salt
- 3 tablespoons extra virgin olive oil
- 3 tablespoons canola oil
- 1 teaspoon crushed red pepper
- A large handful of yarrow leaves, picked from the stem and chopped
- ¼ cup dry white wine
- 4 anchovy filets in oil, rinsed and chopped
- Parmesan cheese

Procedure:

- Mince the yarrow and pepper.
- Boil water and mix in salt.
- Cook pasta in water until it offers a slight resistance when bitten into but is not soft (al dente).
- While the pasta is cooking, heat the oil in the pan with garlic and anchovy filets on low heat until the garlic is fragrant and lightly browned.
- Add the wine to the pan.
- Drain pasta and add to the pan.
- Toss the pasta to coat with the oil and cook for a minute to evaporate any raw wine flavor.
- Add the yarrow mixture and toss just to heat through.
- Garnish with parmesan cheese.

Alternative Usage: Common yarrow has historically been used in traditional medicine as a diaphoretic, astringent, tonic, stimulant, and mild aromatic. The most common use is to stop bleeding and assist in wound healing. Put dry or fresh yarrow leaf on a bleeding wound and hold pressure. It will usually stop the bleeding within 10 to 30 seconds.

Skin Wash

Materials:

- 1 cup crumbled yarrow flower
- Water

Procedure:

- Pour 2 cups of boiling water over a yarrow flower.
- Let steep until cool.
- Strain out flowers.
- Pat wash on the skin.

This wash soothes chapping and minor irritations as well.

Note: Common yarrow may stimulate the uterus, so it is not for use during pregnancy. Those with allergies to ragweed should also avoid it.

Dandelion

Dandelion flower

Dandelion seeds

Scientific Name: *Taraxacum officinale*

Type of Plant: Perennial

Description: Dandelion is one of my favorite plants; it is everywhere and is pretty useful. In my book *52 Unique Techniques for Stocking Food for Preppers*, I used it to make a dandelion wine and described how I first used it as a coffee substitute.

Like other members of the Asteraceae family, dandelions have very small flowers situated together into a composite flower head. Dandelions are tap-rooted herbs and are native to temperate areas of the Northern Hemisphere.

The flower heads are yellow to orange colored, are open in the daytime, and are closed at night.

Natural Range: Dandelions are found on all continents in yards and open areas everywhere.

Food Usage: Roots and leaves have been gathered for food since prehistory, but they are bitter. They are often blanched to remove bitterness or sautéed in the same way as spinach.

Dandelion leaves contain several vitamins and minerals, most notably vitamins A, C, and K, and are also good sources of calcium, potassium, iron, and manganese.

Sautéed Dandelion

Ingredients:

- 3 pounds dandelion greens, tough stems discarded and leaves cut crosswise into 2-inch pieces
- ½ cup extra-virgin olive oil
- 5 large garlic cloves, minced
- ¼ to ½ teaspoon dried hot red pepper flakes
- ½ teaspoon fine sea salt

Preparation:

- Cook greens in a 10- to 12-quart pot of boiling, salted water, uncovered, until ribs are tender (about 10 minutes)
- Drain in a colander, then rinse under cold water and drain, gently pressing out excess water.
- Heat oil in a 12-inch heavy skillet over medium heat.
- Cook garlic and red pepper flakes, stirring, until pale golden, about 45 seconds.
- Increase heat to medium-high.
- Add greens and sea salt.
- Sauté until coated with oil and heated through (about 4 minutes).

Alternative Usage: In almost every culture, the root of the dandelion has been used for the treatment of liver and gallbladder problems, especially the incomplete digestion of fats.

Dandelion Tincture

Use six to twelve drops in juice or water, under the tongue or as desired. It may be taken three times daily to help stimulate urination and bile production and help break down fats.

Materials:

- Fresh clean dandelion roots and leaves
- 90-proof vodka or pure grain alcohol

Procedure:

- Place dandelion pieces in a clean container.
- Add the alcohol at a 2:1 ratio (i.e. 2 cups of vodka to 1 cup of fresh plant material).
- Put the lid on the jar.
- Store the jar in a cool/dry place.
- Shake daily for at least three weeks and up to six months.
- Strain through cheesecloth and compost the herbs.
- Store the tincture in colored dropper bottles or clean glass jars.

Note: Man has eaten dandelion roots going back at least 25,000 years. Check with your doctor before using this or any herb, especially if you have a liver or gallbladder disorder.

Unlike most root plants that are harvested in the fall, dandelion roots should be harvested in the spring.

Eastern Red Cedar (Juniper)

Cedar leaves and berries

Cedar branch

Scientific Name: *Juniperus virginiana*

Type of Plant: Tree

Description: Red cedar is a dense, slow-growing, coniferous evergreen tree that is ordinarily 16 to 66 feet tall, with a short trunk that is one to three feet in diameter. The bark is reddish brown and fibrous, and peels off in narrow strips. The seed cones are less than one-third of an inch long. The seeds are dark purple–blue berries with a white wax cover. The cones contain one to three (rarely up to four) seeds. Thanks to its tolerance of heat, salt, a wide range of soils, and other adverse conditions, the cedar can be put to good use on the farm in windbreaks and in city landscapes for hedges, screens, clumps, or even as specimen trees. It is an aromatic tree, with reddish wood giving off the scent of cedar chests and crushed fruit providing a whiff of the gin they once flavored.

Natural Range: The eastern red cedar tree is a common fixture throughout the plains states and eastern United States. It is mostly found along roads, in fencerows, and scattered across abandoned fields. It especially prefers limestone soils.

Food Usage: The berries are used extensively as a flavoring, and while they can be eaten, their medicinal properties make them too strong for routine consumption. However, the berries can be used to make gin.

Gin

Ingredients:

- 1½ pints 100-proof vodka
- 1½ pints 80-proof vodka
- ¼ cup dried juniper berries
- 2 tablespoons whole coriander, crushed
- 1½ teaspoons dried orange peel
- 1 teaspoon dried lemon peel
- 1 stick whole cinnamon
- 1 whole cardamom pod, crushed
- Activated charcoal filter (A Brita or Berkey filter or something similar works as well.)

Procedure:

- Break up the coriander and cardamom in a food processor or using a mortar and pestle.
- Mix the dry ingredients.
- Place the herbs into a large, sealable jar and add the 100-proof vodka.
- Place the jar in a dark, room-temperature spot for one week.
- Shake at least once a day.
- Strain the mixture through cheesecloth.
- Add 80-proof vodka.
- Pour mixture through a new filter cartridge and repeat 4 additional times.
- Seal in a bottle and drink responsibly.

Alternative Usage: Several studies have shown that red cedar is useful for repelling ticks. One study even found it to be as effective as DEET.

Cedar Insect Repellant
Materials:
• Charcoal
• Dry cedar chips

Procedure:
• Create a smudge by sprinkling dry cedar chips on a charcoal fire.
• Let them smolder to create smoke that works well for repelling insects of all types.

Note: The fine-grained heartwood is fragrant, very light, and very durable, even in contact with soil. Because of this rot resistance, the wood is used for fence posts.

Moths avoid the wood, so it is used as lining for clothes chests and closets.

If prepared properly, it makes excellent English longbows, flat bows, and Native American sinew-backed bows. The best portions of the heartwood are good for making pencils. Juniper oil is distilled from the wood, twigs, and leaves.

Kudzu

Kudzu leaves

Kudzu flower

Scientific Name: *Pueraria lobata*

Type of Plant: Vine

Description: Kudzu is a climbing, semi-woody vine that is related to peas. Its deciduous leaves are composed of three broad leaves that are up to four inches across.

Individual flowers are purple and fragrant and hang in long clusters. The seedpods are brown, hairy, and flat. The pods contain three to ten hard seeds.

Natural Range: Native to Japan, it was introduced into the United States in 1876 to control erosion. Kudzu is very common throughout the Southeast along roadsides and disturbed areas.

Food Usage: The leaves, flowers, and roots are edible. The roots contain a starch that has been used as a foodstuff in Asia for hundreds of years. In Vietnam, the root starch is flavored pomelo oil and is drunk in the summertime. Kudzu root starch can be used as a substitute for cornstarch. The flowers are used to make a jelly that tastes similar to grape jelly, but it is the leaves that we will use in the recipe below.

Rolled Kudzu Leaves

Ingredients:

- 30 medium-sized young kudzu leaves (gathered from an area free of herbicides used to kill kudzu)
- 1 can diced tomatoes
- 2 teaspoons salt
- 3 cloves garlic
- Juice of 3 lemons

Stuffing Ingredients:

- 1 cup rice
- 1 pound ground lamb or lean beef
- 1 cup canned diced tomatoes
- ½ teaspoon of allspice
- Salt and pepper

Procedure:

- Drop leaves into boiling salt water.
- Boil for 2–3 minutes, while gently stirring to separate leaves.
- Remove and place on a plate to cool.
- Cut along stem to middle leaf to remove heavy center.
- Combine all stuffing ingredients and mix well.
- Fill with 1 teaspoon stuffing and roll in the shape of a cigar.
- Place parchment paper or aluminum foil in bottom of a large pan so that rolled leaves will not sit directly on the bottom of the pan.
- Arrange leaf rolls alternately in opposite directions.

- Pour a can of diced tomatoes, 2 teaspoons of salt, and 3 cloves of crushed garlic over the leaves.
- Press down with an inverted dish and add water to reach dish.
- Cover pot and cook on medium for 30 minutes.
- Add lemon juice and cook another 10 minutes.

Alternative Usage: Kudzu has been used as a remedy for alcoholism and hangovers. The root was used to prevent excessive consumption, while the flower was supposed to detoxify the liver and alleviate the symptoms afterwards. In studies, consumption of kudzu tea before drinking caused an increase of intoxication with less total alcohol consumed. It also helps with alcohol cravings, which may be of use during a large-scale disaster when alcohol may not be freely available.

Kudzu Tea

Ingredients:

- 1 cup kudzu leaves, finely chopped
- 1 quart water
- Mint
- Honey

Procedure:

- Simmer the finely chopped Kudzu leaves in a quart of water for 30 minutes.
- Drain and serve with honey and a sprig of mint.
- If you prefer a sweeter tea, add honey to taste.

Note: Many consider kudzu as a takeover plant, because it is hard to eradicate once established and the vines grow several feet in a day. It cannot tolerate shade and does not go deep into wooded areas.

Lamb's Quarters

Lamb's quarters leaves

Lamb's quarters plant

Scientific Name: *Chenopodium album*

Type of Plant: Annual

Description: Lamb's quarters is a rapidly growing summer weed that averages three feet tall. The extremely adaptable growth behavior of lamb's quarters enables the plant to grow in almost any environment. Stems are erect and sturdy and are often tinged red or have pink, purple, or yellow stripes.

Natural Range: Lamb's quarters is found in all inhabited areas of the world except extreme desert climates. It is one of the five most widely distributed plants in the world. It is one of the last weeds to be killed by frost, and its presence is one of the best indicators of good soil.

Food Usage: Lamb's quarters is eaten as a green; however, the flavor is variable due to size of the plant and the growing conditions. They are best eaten when young, because as the leaves mature with age, they gain a greater potency of oxalic acid, which in strong amounts can cause an unpleasant burning sensation in the back of the throat.

Lamb's Quarters Soup

Ingredients:

- 3 tablespoons butter
- 1 small sized onion, chopped
- 3 tablespoons flour
- 1½ teaspoons salt
- Pepper
- 3 cups milk
- About 2 cups cooked, young lamb's quarters, chopped lightly

Procedure:

- Cook up onions in butter until wilted.
- Add flour and cook until mixture browns.
- Add salt and pepper.
- Cook for 3 minutes over medium heat.
- Add milk and lamb's quarters.
- Heat gently.

Alternative Usage: When lamb's quarters leaves are chewed into a paste and applied to the body as a poultice, it works well for insect bites, minor scrapes, inflammation, and sunburn. A tea made from the leaves is beneficial for diarrhea and stomachaches. The tea can also be used as a wash to heal skin irritations and other external complaints.

Lamb's quarters contains saponin, which acts as a mild soap substitute.

Lamb's Quarters Soap Substitute

Ingredients:

- Fresh lamb's quarters roots
- Water

Procedure:

- Clean fresh roots and mash between two rocks.
- Rub roots vigorously with a small amount of water to form light suds.

Note: Lamb's quarters absorbs nitrates readily, so avoid gathering where fertilizer runs off or in other contaminated soil. Also beware of similar plants that have a bad smell. Lamb's quarters does not emit a bad or resinous smell when you crush its leaves between your fingers.

May Apple

May apple plant

May apple fruit

Scientific Name: *Podophyllum peltatum*

Type of Plant: Annual

Description: May apples are woodland plants, typically growing in mature forests in large groups sharing a single root. The stems grow ten to fifteen inches tall, with umbrella-like leaves. Some stems bear a single leaf and do not flower or fruit, while others produce a pair or more leaves with one to eight flowers. The flowers are white, yellow, or red and mature into a green, yellow, or red fleshy fruit one-half to two-thirds of an inch long.

American Basswood (see p. 33)

Birch (see p. 36)

Blackberries (see p. 40)

Cattails (see p. 42)

Comfrey (see p. 44)

Common Yarrow (see p. 47)

Dandelion (see p. 50)

Eastern Red Cedar (Juniper) (see p. 53)

Kudzu (see p. 56)

Lamb's Quarters (see p. 59)

May Apple (see p. 62)

Milk Thistle (see p. 65)

Milkweed (see p. 68)

Mullein (see p. 71)

Oak (see p. 73)

Broadleaf Plantain (see p. 77)

Purslane (see p. 80)

Sassafras (see p. 83)

Shepherd's Purse (see p. 86)

Staghorn Sumac (see p. 89)

Stinging Nettle (see p. 92)

Sycamore (see p. 95)

Walnut (see p. 99)

White Pine (see p. 104)

Willow (see p. 107)

Natural Range: The May apple grows in moist soils in rich woods, thickets, and pastures in Eastern North America from southern Maine to Florida and west to Texas and Minnesota.

Food Usage: All the parts of the plant, except the fruit, are poisonous. The fully ripe fruit is eaten raw or cooked. It can be made into jams, jellies, or pies. May apple seeds and rind are not edible.

May Apple Jelly Recipe
Ingredients:
- 2 cups May apple slices
- 3 cups water
- ⅛ cup lemon juice
- 3½ cups sugar
- 3 ounces liquid fruit pectin

Procedure:
- Wash ripe May apples and cut away stem, blossom ends, and any discolored or damaged areas.
- Remove seeds and rind.
- Cut fruit into pieces and place in large kettle with water to cover.
- Bring to a boil, then simmer until fruit is tender, mashing during cooking.
- Strain juice through cheesecloth (2 cups of fruit should result in at least 1 ¾ cups juice).
- Add lemon juice and sugar to strained juice.
- Bring mixture to a boil, stirring in the liquid fruit pectin.
- Continue to boil and stir constantly until "jelly stage" is reached.
- Remove jelly from heat, skim foam from top, and pour into hot, sterilized jelly glasses.
- Seal at once with lid, and process jars in hot water bath. For half pints or pint jars, process for 5 minutes at altitudes from 0 to 1,000 feet; 10 minutes for altitudes from 1,001 to 6,000 feet; and 15 minutes for altitudes above 6,000 feet.

Alternative Usage: May apple can be also used topically for warts, and some over-the-counter treatments for genital warts contains chemicals found in May apple roots.

Podophyllum resin obtained from the root is the only part of the plant used in herbal medicine.

May Apple Wart Tincture*

Materials:
- Fresh May apple root
- 190-proof grain alcohol

Procedure:
- Finely chop or grind clean herb to release juice and expose surface area.
- Fill jar ¼ to ½ with roots.
- Completely cover roots with alcohol.
- Jar should appear full of roots but should move freely when shaken.
- Store jar in a cool, dry, dark cabinet.
- Shake several times a week.
- If the alcohol has evaporated a bit and the herb is not totally submerged, be sure to top off the jar with more alcohol.
- Allow the mixture to extract for 6–8 weeks.
- Drape a damp cheesecloth over a funnel. Pour contents of tincture into an amber glass bottle. Allow to drip, then squeeze and twist until all liquid is removed.

Note: The ripened fruit is edible in small amounts but is poisonous when consumed in large amounts. The rhizome, foliage, and roots are also poisonous. May apple contains podophyllotoxin, which has a number of medical applications.

---

*Use topically in small areas for short durations. Long-term or large-scale use can result in poisoning.

Milk Thistle

Milk thistle

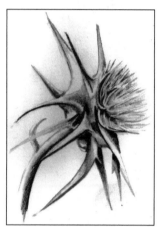

Thistle flower

Scientific Name: *Silybum marianum*

Type of Plant: Annual

Description: Milk thistle is a stout plant that grows up to one yard tall and has a branched stem. It can easily be identified by its uniquely shaped flower and prickly stem. Milk thistle flower heads are light purple in color. They flower from June to August in the Northern Hemisphere or December to February in the Southern Hemisphere.

Natural Range: Milk thistle is grown worldwide and in some countries is considered an invasive weed. It is interesting to note that milk thistle is also grown in large amounts on commercial farms due to its medical use.

Food Usage: Milk thistle has been used as food. Personally, I use it (and wrote about it in *52 Unique Techniques for Stocking Food for Preppers*) to make vegetable rennet for cheese. The roots can be eaten raw or boiled, parboiled, or roasted. The young shoots in spring can be cut down to the root and boiled. The spiny bracts on the flower head can be eaten like globe artichoke (which it is related to), and the stems (after peeling) can be soaked overnight and stewed.

How to Prepare Milk Thistle Stalks for Eating

Ingredients:
• Milk thistle stalk

Procedure:
• Turn thistle stalk over and make an incision with a knife near the base of the stalk, cutting through the stalk toward the leaves. Do not cut completely through. By cutting the stalk, you can peel the leaves away.
• Once the thorny leaves are peeled away, scrape out the fiber in the center of the stalk. This leaves a stalk that looks like celery.
• Cut into smaller segments and enjoy raw with a dip as you would celery stalks, or add to salads, stir fry, or boil.

Alternative Usage: Milk thistle contains silymarin, a strong liver medicine. The use of milk thistle to help with liver function is one of the few herbal medicines accepted by modern medicine. It has been used to help with cirrhosis of the liver caused by alcoholism and has been studied for treatment of hepatitis.

Milk Thistle Tea

Ingredients:
• 1 tablespoon milk thistle seeds
• 3 cups water

Procedure:
• Crush milk thistle seeds.
• Add to water and boil.
• Steep for about 20 minutes and strain.

Drink one cup 30 minutes before meals in the morning, afternoon, and evening, as well as just before going to bed. After two to three days, reduce your intake to three times a day.

Note: Some medical research suggests that milk thistle, combined with traditional treatment, can improve diabetes. Studies have shown a decrease in blood sugar levels as well as help with insulin resistance in people with type 2 diabetes.

Milkweed

Milkweed leaf

Milkweed pod

Scientific Name: *Asclepias L*

Type of Plant: Perennial

Description: Milkweed grows up to six feet tall. It has large, broad leaves, usually four to ten inches long. They sometimes have red veins. When the pods are crushed, they release a milky sap that the milkweed is named for.

Natural Range: This plant is found in fields, gardens, and along roads throughout the United States (except for the Pacific Northwest).

Food Usage: The boiled young shoots, leaves, unopened flower buds, flowers, and young pods are edible and most often consumed as cooked greens, cooked vegetables, or fritters.

Sautéed Milkweed Pods

Ingredients:

- Two dozen small, whole milkweed pods, each shorter than 2 inches in length
- 1 to 1½ cups all-purpose flour
- 2 tablespoons unsalted butter
- 1 tablespoon olive oil
- Salt and pepper

Procedure:

- Place pods in a 4-quart saucepan and cover with cold water.
- Bring to a boil, and boil pods for 10 minutes.
- Drain and repeat the boiling process one more time.
- Place one cup of flour in a plastic bag.
- Place 6 pods in the bag and shake to coat with flour.
- Spread coated pods on a towel. Repeat until all of the pods are coated.
- In a large skillet, melt the butter in the oil.
- Add pods and allow them to cook without stirring for 3–4 minutes until the undersides form a golden crust.
- Stir and cook another 3 to 5 minutes until the pods are tender.
- Season with sea salt and pepper.

Alternative Usage: The fine milkweed fibers are great for making cordage.

Milkweed String

Material:

- Milkweed plant

Procedure:

- Harvest the plant and let it dry.
- Break up the stalk and pull long pieces off it and set them aside.

- "Thigh-roll" the pieces to make cord:
- Use two small bunches of fibers that are of different length.
- Hold the ends of two in your left hand.
- Drape their other ends over your right thigh.
- Roll the strands down your thigh using the palm and thumb of your right hand so that the strands "S" twist up.
- At the end of the roll, release the hold of your left hand on the fibers and allow the strands to "Z" twist in the opposite direction.
- To make even string, continually splice new strands of fiber every couple of inches.
- To splice in a length of fiber, lay the new piece along the shorter of the two original strands.
- Twist the new and original fiber together as one strand and continue rolling the cordage. Each time a new piece is spliced in, leave an inch or so of the new fiber projecting from the plied cord, these can be trimmed off when the cord is finished.

Note: The milkweed filaments are hollow and coated with wax and have good insulation qualities. During World War II, over 5,000 tons of milkweed floss was collected in the United States as a substitute for kapok in flotation vests.

Milkweed is grown commercially as a hypoallergenic filling for pillows.

The fibers of some species can be used for cordage.

Milkweed is beneficial to nearby plants, repelling some pests, especially wireworms.

Mullein

Mullein plant

Mullein flower

Scientific Name: *Verbascum*

Type of Plant: Perennial

Description: Mullein grows from ½ to 10 feet tall. Young plants start as a dense rosette of leaves at ground level and send up a tall flowering stem as they grow. The leaves are spirally arranged and densely hairy, although some species of mullein are hairless. The flowers have five symmetrical petals; petal colors include yellow, orange, reddish brown, purple, blue, or white. The fruit is a capsule that contains many tiny seeds.

Natural Range: Mullein can be found growing in open fields, waste places, disturbed areas, railway embankments, and similar dry, sunny localities.

Food Usage: The leaves and flowers are edible, but making tea from them is preferable to eating them in a salad.

Mullein Tea

Ingredients:

- 6 large mullein leaves
- 5 cups water
- Honey (if desired)

Procedure:

- Break leaves into small pieces.
- Add boiling water.
- Let the tea steep for 5 minutes.
- Serve.

Alternative Usage: While mullein tea is a traditional treatment for respiratory problems, mullein has another vital use. It is also known as cowboy toilet paper. While I don't feel the need to go into detailed instructions for using a leaf for toiletry purposes, I will say that you should use the leaf in a direction that flows with the hairs, and you should test your skin with the leaf because it does cause nausea or contact dermatitis in some people.

Note: The stalk of the plant is a good drill for use in the hand-drill method of friction fire lighting.

Oak

Oak leaf

Oak acorn

Scientific Name: *Quercus robur*

Type of Plant: Tree

Description: There are approximately 600 species of oaks. Oaks have spirally arranged leaves and some have serrated leaves or entire leaves with smooth edges. Oak trees produce an acorn nut that is edible, even though most species of oaks produce acorns with a high level of tannin, requiring processing before the acorn is palatable.

Natural Range: Oak trees are native to the Northern Hemisphere and include deciduous and evergreen species that are widely disbursed in North, Central, and South Americas, Asia, Europe, and North Africa. There are over ninety different types of oak trees in the United States alone.

Food Usage: Acorns are edible, but many acorns need to be processed to remove the bitter-tasting tannin compound from the nuts. In my book *52 Prepper Projects*, I showed how to process the nuts and use them as a flour substitute. The process is simple. Remove the nut meat from the shell by breaking the hard outer coating and picking the nutmeat out. Then soak the nut in water for several hours. When the water takes on a dark color, pour it off and replace the water. Do this until the water is clear or the nuts taste palatable to you. Once the acorns are leached, they can be dried a bit to grind into flour or used while the chunks are still damp.

Roasted Acorns

Ingredients:

- Leached acorns
- Salt

Procedure:

- Place the damp nut chunks on a baking sheet and sprinkle with salt.
- Toast them for 15–20 minutes at 375ºF in an oven.
- The nuts are ready when the color has darkened slightly and the nut pieces smell like roasted nuts.

Alternative Usage: The tannic acid removed from the acorns (or harvested from oak wood bark and chips) can be used to vegetable tan leather.

Vegetable Tanning Hide

Materials

- 30 gallons tannic acid (dark water gathered from boiling acorns, oak bark, and oak chips)
- 4-pound bag of hydrated lime (Garden stores sell this, but I have a article on my website (tngun.com) showing how to make this from limestone.)

- 5 gallons fresh chicken or cow manure
- Water
- 100 percent neatsfoot oil
- Small piece of beeswax

Procedure:

- The flesh side of the hide is scraped with a dull knife to remove any traces of flesh, blood, and fat.
- Once the hide has been thoroughly scraped, wash it off.
- Put approximately 15 gallons of water in a large plastic garbage can.
- Mix in hydrated lime and stir well.
- Put the hide in the liquid and churn for two or three days. The hair will start slipping out of the hide when the hide is ready.
- Remove the hide and scrape the hair side to remove the hair.
- Rinse hide in a plastic tub with 8 or 9 changes of water.
- Mix manure with enough water to make a medium slurry and dump the mix and the hide in the plastic tub.
- Stir the hide constantly for 30 minutes and let set for another 3 or 4 days with occasional stirring.
- This manure process is called bating and makes the hide soft. When the bating process is done, rinse the hide very well using 12 or 13 changes of water and scrape both sides until the hide is clean and smooth.
- Place the hide in the tub filled with the tannic acid bath, stir for 15 minutes, and let sit for a week, stirring every few hours. If the mix starts to ferment with a sulfur-like smell, dump in a half gallon of white vinegar into the mix.
- After 3 weeks, dump out the mix and refresh with more tannic acid. Repeat the process for an additional 6 weeks.
- Repeat the process with a very strong and dark tannic acid bath and let the leather sit for 3 months.
- Take the leather out of the vat and rinse 12 or more times in clean water.
- Place the hide on a hard surface and use a piece of smooth, hard wood to squeegee out the water, but do not let it dry.
- Heat up 100 percent pure neatsfoot oil and melt some beeswax into it.
- Let cool and work it deeply into the hair side of the hide.
- Flip it over and let the hide slowly dry over a couple of days.
- Occasionally work the leather by pulling and stretching it.

- Once dry, dampen the leather slightly, warm your oil and beeswax mix, and rub it into the flesh side of the leather.
- Work the leather as it dries, and when done you will have leather tanned much like the leather of the American pioneers.

Note: Not all acorns require leaching of tannin. Indian tribes have fought wars over sweet oaks that were especially prolific, as an oak can produce thousand of acorns with an acre of oak trees producing more than a quarter ton of nut meat.

Broadleaf Plantain

Plantain leaf

Plantain plant

Scientific Name: *Plantago major*

Type of Plant: Perennial

Description: Broadleaf plantain is a perennial herb that grows from a rosette of leaves that are six inches to one foot long. Each oval-shaped leaf is two to eight inches long and one and a half to four inches wide. The flowers are small, are brown with a purplish tent, and have purple stamens, which are produced in a dense spike two to six inches long on top of a stem five to six inches tall.

Natural Range: Broadleaf plantain is native to most of Europe and northern and central Asia, but it has spread widely throughout the world.

Food Usage: Broadleaf plantain is a very nutritious wild food. It is high in calcium and vitamins A, C, and K. The leaves are edible as a salad green when young and tender, but they quickly become tough and fibrous as they get older. However, the older leaves can be stewed to tenderize.

Pan-Fried Plantain and Onions
Ingredients:

- 3 cups fresh plantain leaves
- 1 diced medium onion
- 2 tablespoons olive oil
- 2 sliced bell peppers
- 2 tablespoons apple cider vinegar
- Salt and pepper

Procedure:

1. Pour 1 tablespoon olive oil into pan and heat to medium high.
2. Add onion and pepper and cook until onion is translucent.
3. Add the plantain leaves and the rest of the oil.
4. Cook until you get the desired tenderness (too much heat will cause the leaves to disintegrate—I feel that 3–5 minutes is best).
5. Add the apple cider vinegar and a pinch of salt and pepper.

Alternative Usage: It is one of the most abundant and widely distributed medicinal crops in the world. A poultice of the leaves can be applied to wounds, stings, and sores in order to facilitate healing and prevent infection. Plantain tea has been used to treat diarrhea and dysentery, both because the astringent properties help resolve the issue and because the high vitamin and mineral content replaces the nutrients lost during the illness. It has also been suggested that since the aucubin found in plantain leaves leads to increased uric acid excretion from the kidneys, it may be useful in treating gout.

Plantain Healing Salve
Ingredients:

- 1 pound chopped plantain (entire plant)
- 1 cup lard

Procedure:

- In a large non-metallic pan, mix chopped plantain and lard.
- Cover.
- Cook on low heat until the leaves turn to mush.
- Strain while hot into an airtight container (I like to use small half-pint jelly jars).
- Cool.

While this works well on first-degree burns, insect bites, rashes, and sores, it is also useful as a nighttime wrinkle cream.

Note: The fiber from the mature plant is both pliable and tough, which makes it a great candidate for use as survival cordage.

Purslane

Purslane

Purslane flower

Scientific Name: *Portulaca oleracea*

Type of Plant: Annual

Description: Purslane has smooth, reddish stems that mostly lie on the ground. The stem has alternate leaves that cluster at both the stem ends and joints. The flowers are yellow, have five regular parts, and are up to a quarter-inch wide. The flowers may appear regardless of the season depending on rainfall, but they only open for a few hours on sunny mornings.

Natural Range: Purslane grows in orchards, vineyards, crop fields, gardens, roadsides, and other disturbed sites throughout the United States. It can live in compacted soils and is very tolerant of both poor soil and drought conditions due to its taproot and strong secondary roots.

Food Usage: Purslane contains omega-3s and beta-carotene plus vitamin C in its stems. It tastes similar to spinach and can be substituted for it in most recipes.

Purslane Pesto

Ingredients:

- One large handful of purslane with the stems removed
- ⅔ cup walnuts
- ¼ cup olive oil
- Juice from half a lemon
- 2 teaspoons honey
- Sea salt and pepper

Procedure:

- Place all ingredients in a food processor and pulse until you can't see any whole leaves.
- Use it on toasted bread, pizza, or with pasta.

Alternative Usage: Purslane has several medicinal properties. It will reduce the side effects of too much caffeine, it is thought to help stabilize blood sugar, it can bolster your immune system, and the high levels of magnesium are said to reduce migraine headache frequency and help lower blood pressure.

King Henry VIII of England used purslane tea to help relieve the symptoms of gout. He drank several cups of the tea about an hour after heavy meals.

Purslane Tea

Ingredients:

- 12 cups chopped purslane leaves
- ½ cup chopped chickweed leaves
- 3 cups boiling water

Procedure:

- Combine purslane and chickweed.
- Steep in boiling water for 5 minutes.
- Drink.

Note: Although purslane is considered a weed in the United States, it has more omega-3 acids per gram than almost any other plant. Half a cup of purslane leaves contains 300–400 mg of the essential fatty acid (8.5 mg per gram).

Sassafras

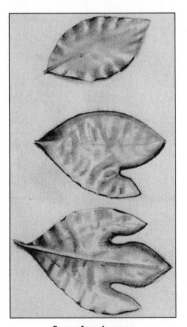

Sassafras leaves

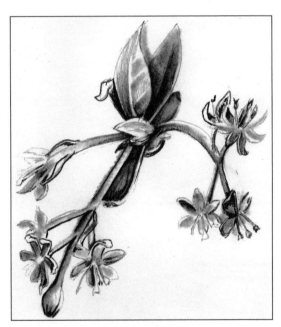

Sassafras flower

Scientific Name: *Sassafras albidum*

Type of Plant: Tree

Description: As a child who grew up as the son of a state park ranger, sassafras is one of the first trees I learned to identify. I found the sassafras to be easy to identify because it has three different types of leaf patterns. It has an oval leaf, a mitten-shaped leaf, and a three-pronged leaf. This makes it almost impossible to misidentify. The sassafras tree grows 30 to 115 feet tall, has many slender branches, and has a smooth bark. The young leaves and twigs produce a citrus scent when crushed.

Natural Range: Sassafras ranges from southern Maine and southern Ontario, west to Iowa, and south to central Florida and eastern Texas. It is most often found in open woods, along fencerows, or in fields. It thrives in moist, well-drained, or sandy loam soils and tolerates a variety of soil types.

Food Usage: If you have ever eaten filé gumbo, you have eaten sassafras. While okra is used as a thickening agent in traditional Louisiana gumbo, okra does not keep well, so filé powder made from sassafras is used instead. In all actuality, I like filé gumbo better.

Filé Powder

Ingredients:

• Sassafras
• Bay leaf (optional)

Procedure:

• Locate a sassafras tree and cut several branches containing young tender leaves.
• Hang the branches outside but out of direct sunlight for a week or until dry.
• When the leaves are completely dry, remove the leaves from the stems.
• Pulverize leaves with a mortar and pestle until very finely powdered.
• Pass the powder through a very fine sieve.
• Store in an airtight container and keep out of the sunlight.
• Use sparingly as too much filé in your gumbo will turn it to thick sludge. Also, you should wait to add it the end of the cooking process, as too much heat will make it bitter and unappetizing.

Alternative Usage: The American Indians use sassafras as a medicinal herb. It was used it in teas and poultices to reduce fever, gout, rheumatism, eye inflammation, and scurvy. Sassafras contains safrole oil, which gives sassafras its unique flavor. This flavor made sassafras a main ingredient in root beer. Unfortunately, safrole oil was regulated in 1976 because the FDA found that it causes cancer in lab rats when ingested in large amounts.

Safrole oil kills hair lice, so a strong tea made from sassafras roots makes an effective hair wash if you need to remove lice.

Sassafras Hair Wash

Ingredients:
- 1 cup sassafras root bark
- 3 cups boiling water

Procedure:
- Place bark in a pot.
- Pour a cup of boiling water over bark.
- Let it steep for 20 minutes.
- Cool.
- Wash hair with the strong tea.
- This mixture is too strong to be used as a tea. A better tea recipe for consumption would be closer to 1 teaspoon of root to a cup of water.

Note: The FDA did regulate sassafras; however, upon further study I found that the test method used petroleum-based products to dissolve the safrole (which is not water soluble) and that rats have an enzyme (that people don't have) that helps in the process. While I am not a doctor, and am not suggesting you do or do not ingest anything containing safrole oil, I am not convinced that a glass of sassafras tea occasionally imbibed as a spring tonic is dangerous.

What I found interesting is that safrole is used to make MDMA, which means the US federal government regulates and tracks sassafras extract due to illicit ecstasy labs. I conclude that the real reason root beer is not made with sassafras is not health-related but is rather part of the war on drugs.

Shepherd's Purse

Shepherd's purse

Shepherd's purse flower

Scientific Name: *Capsella bursa-pastoris*

Type of Plant: Annual

Description: Shepherd's purse is named from its triangular, purse-like pods. The plant is a small annual plant related to mustard. Unlike most flowering plants, shepherd's purse flowers year-round, making it capable of producing several generations a year.

Shepherd's purse grows from a rosette of lobed leaves on the ground. A foot-long stem grows from this base. The flowers are small and white and produce heart-shaped seed pods.

Natural Range: Shepherd's purse is native to Eastern Europe and Asia Minor, but is naturalized through the world. Its ability to rapidly reseed causes it to be considered a weed in many places. It grows on disturbed soil, in untended meadows and lawns, and along roadsides and trails.

Food Usage: Shepherd's purse is used as a very mild mustard green. It contains vitamins C, A, and K, some protein, as well as sulfur, calcium, iron, potassium, and sodium. They shrink about 75 percent when cooked.

Shepherd's Purse Butter

Ingredients:

- 3½ ounces butter
- ½ cup Shepherd's purse leaves, chopped
- 1 garlic clove
- 10 capers
- 2 anchovies
- 1 hard-boiled egg
- 1 egg yolk
- 1½ tablespoons vinegar
- Salt and pepper

Procedure:

- Rinse the capers and wash the greens carefully.
- Blend all the ingredients together in a blender.

This compound butter is really good on fish.

Alternative Usage: When dried and infused, shepherd's purse tea is considered by herbalists as one of the best solutions for stopping hemorrhages of all kinds when given in the form of a fluid extract, in doses of one to two teaspoons.

Women may use shepherd's purse for premenstrual problems, long periods, and menstrual cramps in moderate doses of one-quarter to one-half teaspoon at a time—up to one teaspoonful—three or four times a day before the menstrual period is due and during the period to reduce heavy bleeding.

Shepherd's Purse Tea

Ingredients:

- 2 tablespoons dried shepherd's purse leaves
- 1 pint water

Procedure:

- Boil the water.
- Put two tablespoonsful of dried shepherd's purse into boiling water.
- Cover the container and remove it from the heat.
- Allow tea to steep for 45 minutes.
- Filter the liquid and store it in a refrigerator. It is best to take this tea when it is cool.

Note: The ingestion of shepherd's purse is not recommended for use during pregnancy because of its ability to cause uterine contractions. Do not take long-term but rather to treat systems as the astringent properties can increase blood pressure.

Staghorn Sumac

Staghorn sumac leaf

Staghorn sumac berry cluster

Scientific Name: *Rhus typhina*

Type of Plant: Tree

Description: Sumac is a deciduous shrub or small tree growing to 15 feet tall. It has alternate, pinnately compound leaves 10 to 22 inches long, with 9 to 31 serrate leaflets each. The stalk that attaches the leaf blade to the stem is densely covered in rust-colored hairs. Staghorn sumac is most easily identified by its fruit, which sits in dense clusters of small red drupes at the end of the branches.

These clusters are conical, four to eight inches long, and approximately two inches across at the base. The plant flowers from May to July and the fruit ripens from June to September. The fruit has been known to last through winter and into spring.

Natural Range: Staghorn Sumac is found mostly in the eastern United States. It is a common sight along highways and rural routes throughout the southern United States.

Food Usage: The sumac is best known for a tart tea made from soaking the berries in cold water. This drink is high in vitamin C and is a nice summertime treat. Sumac is used as a spice in many Middle Eastern areas. Ground sumac berries create a spice that has a tangy flavor that is similar to, but less tart than, lemon juice. It's best sprinkled over foods before serving but can be used in marinades and dressings.

While it is great over vegetables and hummus, it really shines when used on meat.

Sumac Dry Rub

Ingredients:

- 5 tablespoons sea salt
- 4 tablespoons black pepper
- 2 tablespoons part sumac
- 2 tablespoons garlic powder
- 2 tablespoons ground coffee
- 1 tablespoon cocoa powder
- 1 tablespoon brown sugar

Procedure:

- Mix ingredients well to make 1 cup of rub.
- You will need approximately ¼ cup of rub mix per steak.
- Apply a generous amount of rub to one side of steak.
- Using your hand, rub the spices into the meat until it is fully covered.
- Turn steak over and repeat.
- Cover the meat and let it rest in the refrigerator overnight.
- Let the meat come to room temperature prior to grilling it.
- Put the steaks on a preheated grill and cook to your taste.

Alternative Usage: Sumac is used as a dye as well as being a natural mordant. A mordant sets dyes in the fabric so that they do not wash out. While you should always test a small piece of scrap of the fabric you are using when using natural plant dyes so you won't be surprised, the following recipe should produce a nice burgundy color when used with 100 percent cotton.

Sumac Dye
Ingredients:

- Cotton
- 2 gallons sumac berries
- 1 gallon water

Procedure:

- Cover the berries with 1 gallon of water and boil for an hour.
- When dye is desired strength, strain dye thoroughly because any loose berries will cause a dark patch on the cloth.
- Immerse cotton, adding water if necessary.
- Boil for at least 30 minutes and until fabric is the desired shade.
- Rinse in cold water.
- Dry.

Be aware that an ingredient in modern detergents causes the fabric to change color to a grayish green, so only wash with water unless you've tested the soap first.

Note: Some beekeepers use dried sumac bobs as a source of fuel for their smokers.

Staghorn sumac is not to be confused with poison sumac. Nonpoisonous sumac has red berries. Green or yellow berries are from the poisonous variety and should not be used.

Stinging Nettle

Stinging nettle

Stinging nettle flower

Scientific Name: *Urtica dioica*

Type of Plant: Perennial

Description: Stinging nettle is a plant that I have seeded into the land behind my back fence. I have done this because of the usefulness of the plant, but

I have to admit I did run into some trouble with my neighbors when I was deciding what types of plants to seed in a permaculture-type food forest.

Singing nettle has many hollow stinging hairs on the leaves and stems. These hairs act like hypodermic needles that inject histamine and other chemicals, causing a stinging sensation when contacted by humans and other animals. The nettle grows three to seven feet tall during the summer but dies down to the ground during the winter. The leaves are one to six inches long and grow oppositely on a wiry stem. The leaves have a strongly serrated edge. The numerous flowers are small with a green or brown tint.

Natural Range: Nettles are native to Europe, Asia, and northern Africa, as well as western North America. In the United States, it is found in every state except for Hawaii. It grows best in places with high annual rainfall.

Food Usage: While the stinging nettle has fine hairs on the leaves and stems that shoot painful chemicals into the skin when touched, it is a wild edible with several uses. Nettles are best eaten as a cooked green as cooking destroys the painful chemicals, but be sure to wear gloves when you are harvesting stinging nettle. You can also use nettles for any baked recipe that calls for spinach.

Nettle Greens

Ingredients:
- 2 or 3 handfuls stinging nettle leaves
- ¼ cup of Parmesan cheese
- Salt and pepper

Procedure:
- Rinse nettles in a colander then toss in a pot with lid, leaving water on the leaves.
- Cook on medium high heat 2–4 minutes or until tender.
- Sprinkle with Parmesan and salt and pepper.

Alternative Usage: Stinging nettle works just like thistle to coagulate milk so you can make cheese. As with thistle, this vegetarian rennet will impart a bitter flavor to aged cheese, so it is not recommended for cheeses that require an aging process longer than two months.

Nettle Rennet

Ingredients:

- 2 lbs. fresh nettle leaves
- Water
- Sea salt

Procedure:

- Rinse fresh leaves.
- Fill a large pot with 4 cups water.
- Add the clean leaves.
- Add more water if needed to just cover the nettle leaves.
- Bring the water and leaves to a light boil.
- Reduce heat, cover, and simmer 30 minutes.
- Add 1 heaping tablespoon of sea salt to the pot.
- Stir gently to dissolve.
- Place a colander inside a large bowl.
- Line the colander with one layer of clean cheesecloth.
- Pour nettles into colander.
- Collect the water by draining until leaves stop dripping.

The liquid drained from the nettle leaves is the liquid nettle rennet. It can be used in amounts of one cup of nettle rennet to one gallon of warmed milk. If kept cold and away from light, it will keep for a few weeks.

Note: Stinging nettle tea can be used as a rinse for the hair to help restore color and aid with hair growth. Nettles are used by the beauty industry to create anti-dandruff and scalp products.

Sycamore

Sycamore leaf

Sycamore seed pod

Scientific Name: *Platanus occidentalis*

Type of Plant: Tree

Description: Sycamores are easy to identify because their bark flakes off in large irregular masses. This molting causes the tree trunk to have a mottled look with splotches of greenish white, gray, and brown. A sycamore can grow 100 to 130 feet high and five to six and a half feet in diameter. The sycamore tree often divides near the ground into several trunks, and the trunks of large trees are often hollow.

Natural Range: The sycamore often grows near rivers and in wetland areas. Its native territory is quite extensive in the United States, as it ranges throughout the Eastern United States and the Midwest. Because it is sometimes grown for timber, it has been planted outside its native range.

Food Usage: While not as common as maple sugaring, the process of collecting sycamore sap has been known for hundreds of years. It is very easy to collect. Sycamore sap can be drunk straight from the collection can, fermented into a drink, or condensed down into syrup. A healthy sycamore produces one gallon of sap per day at the height of the sap run, and the season is generally a month long. Sap flows best on days that are above freezing following nights during which the temperature had dropped below freezing. One thing to note when deciding what to do with your sap is that it takes ten gallons of sap to condense into a quart of syrup, so you will need ten or more trees to gather any appreciable amount. However, it is a fairly easy process.

Collecting Sycamore Sap

Materials:

- Drill and 7/16 drill bit
- ½ inch vinyl tubing
- Collection jugs (Water jugs are fine, but thicker plastic is better as long as it is food safe.)

Procedure:

- Find sycamores at least one foot in diameter. Large trees can hold more than one tap, but sometimes the tree is more productive with less taps, and too many can potentially damage the tree.
- Drill a hole three inches deep on the south side of each tree.
- Angle your bit slightly upward as you drill to encourage the sap to drain.
- Clean out each drill hole to remove any shavings.
- Insert one end of the tubing into the hole and the other end into the container.
- Collect your sap each day to avoid overflowing containers.

Condensing Sycamore Syrup

Materials:

- Steady heat source (A wood fire is fine, but I prefer a propane fryer.)
- Large pot
- Lots of sap

Procedure:

- Do this project outside, as you will be boiling the water from the sap, which will cause condensation
- Bring the sap to a boil and keep it boiling until it visibly thickens.
- Dip a spoon into the syrup and pull out one spoonful.
- Allow it to cool for a moment and then see how it pours. If the syrup forms a curtain-like sheet off the spoon edge, then you are done.
- If it is runny, keep boiling.
- Keep your finished syrup refrigerated or can in a water bath canner for longer storage.

Alternative Usage: Sycamore is not the best wood for many types of woodworking projects as it is coarse-grained and difficult to work with, but when carved green, it has been used extensively for butcher blocks and food utensils.

When dry or nearly dry it can be very hard, so it is best to do the carving, especially the roughing out, while green.

Tips for Spoon Carving

- Always make sure you use a maximum of half but preferably only a quarter of the log or less. This reduces splitting problems.
- Make sure not to include the pith in any part of your carving.
- Be careful not to make the neck of the spoon too thin.
- Leave your spoon block in water when done for the day.
- Once a spoon is carved just let it dry. It is not necessary to wrap it in anything; just do not dry rapidly or subject to heat while drying.
- If you need to keep the spoon green either leave in a plastic bag or place it in the freezer.

Carving a Spoon

- Draw the top profile of your spoon on a block of wood—the grain should run along the long end.
- Remove as much wood as possible from the block to come close to your drawn edge.

- Using a sharp knife, carefully carve right to your line all the way around the block.
- Sketch the side profile of your spoon on the block.
- Using a sharp knife, remove wood to match your design.
- If you have a crooked knife, you probably don't need a tutorial, but if you want to buy one, it makes it simple to carve out the bowl. Use your thumb and finger to judge thickness of the bowl and go slow so you do not carve a hole through it.
- If you can't or don't want to buy a hook knife, you can cheat and use a small burning ember to slowly burn away a depression. Go slowly and carefully, as too much heat can cause your wood to crack. I have used this process to make bowls. Simply set a glowing ember on the wood you wish to char away and blow on it through a metal straw (a small piece of copper tube is the easiest to use). As the wood chars, scrape it away with a knife or a piece of glass.
- Once the bowl is carved, sand the spoon smooth.
- Let dry.
- Coat the spoon with edible oil like olive or walnut oil.

Note: Sycamore is a good wood to use as a wood drill when lighting a fire by friction. It also works well as firewood as it produces a hot flame and strong embers.

Walnut

Walnut leaf

Walnut seed in husk

Scientific Name: *Juglans*

Type of Plant: Tree

Description: Walnut trees are trees with a wide-spreading canopy. The trunk of the tree can reach over six and a half feet in diameter and 115 feet in height.

Mature walnut trees have a smooth silver-gray bark. Its bright green leaves have an odd number of smaller oval leaflets. The inedible fleshy green fruit of the walnut tree contains the edible nut.

Natural Range: Found throughout the eastern United States, black walnut is found naturally growing from Vermont to Minnesota and south to Florida and Texas. It thrives in deep, well-drained soils. It is a shade-intolerant tree and must have direct sunlight to grow.

Food Usage: The primary food usage is the walnut. While the hard nut casing has antioxidants that help keep the nut oil from going rancid, the walnut must be stored properly to keep out insect and mold infestations. Because fungal mold creates aflatoxin, any mold in a walnut batch ruins the entire store. For home storage the nuts should be kept under low humidity and between the temperatures of 27°F to 32°F. Walnut meat may be candied, pickled, used raw, roasted, cooked or baked, or turned into nut butter. I am fortunate in that I have several walnut trees near my house and get buckets of walnuts each year, so when researching what projects and recipes to use for this book, I was able to try a lot of things for this particular tree. I could not narrow the food project down to one item, so I decided to throw in a bonus recipe. We are going to show how to not only roast walnuts but also how to cook them in pasta sauce.

Roast Walnuts

Ingredients:

• Walnuts
• Nut oil (optional but it makes a difference)
• Salt (optional)

Procedure:

• Preheat oven to 350°F.
• Spread the nuts in an even layer on the baking sheet.
• If you decide to use oil, use as little oil as possible. Drizzle a couple of teaspoons of oil over the nuts and toss to coat.
• Place tray in oven and roast for 5 minutes.
• Remove after 5 minutes, stir, and return tray to oven.
• Check the nuts again after 3 minutes. The nuts are done when the color is darker and they smell nutty. You may hear them crackling. The process should take only 8–12 minutes.

- Remove from the oven and immediately transfer onto a plate or another baking sheet to cool. They may scorch if you leave them in the hot tray.
- Sprinkle salt on roasted nuts while they are hot. I don't normally do this, but I have on occasion roasted nuts with honey.

Additional tips for roasting walnuts: Roasting nuts with a touch of oil is a really nice way to add flavor and crispness. Personally, I love oil-roasted nuts for snacking, but it does add oil, so be careful with this if you plan on using the nuts in a recipe.

Close care must be taken as they can go from done to burnt in less than a minute. Smaller nuts cook faster than larger nuts, so the preheating is critical to a good result.

Chop the nuts after roasting them. Chopped nuts burn extremely easy and roasted nuts chop easier and with less flaking.

Bonus Recipe:

Pasta with Walnut Sauce

Ingredients:

- 6 ounces roasted walnuts
- ½ clove garlic, minced
- 1 slice bread, crusts removed
- ⅔ cup whole milk
- 1 ounce grated Parmesan
- 3–4 tablespoons olive oil
- Salt and pepper
- 2 pounds any flat pasta broken into short lengths (tagliatelle, fettuccine, pappardelle, linguine all work well)

Procedure:

- Boil a large saucepan of water.
- Put bread in a bowl and cover with milk.
- Blend the toasted walnuts (reserve 1 ounce for later), garlic, bread soaked in milk, and Parmesan until the mix becomes smooth and creamy.
- Pour the oil in the blender and season with salt and pepper and blend the mixture again.
- Pour into a bowl, and set aside.

- Add pasta to boiling water with salt and cook until the pasta is al dente.
- Reserve a cup of the pasta cooking liquid.
- Drain the pasta and place in a large bowl while it is still dripping water.
- Sprinkle some olive oil over the pasta to prevent it from sticking together.
- Add walnut sauce, mixing it into the pasta (if the sauce is too thick, add a small amount of pasta water as needed).
- Add remaining walnuts and Parmesan to pasta as a garnish.

Alternative Usage: Walnut stains everything. If you have ever husked walnuts without gloves, you probably had black-dyed hands for weeks. I have a friend who is a very experienced trapper (see the dedication to the book), and he has used walnuts to dye his snares and traps. Dried walnut husks have been used as ink. Leonardo da Vinci and Rembrandt used walnut ink for their work because it lasts so long. Walnuts have been used as hair dye in ancient Rome and medieval Europe. When used with fabric, walnut makes a colorfast, wash- and light-resistant brown earth tone dye. This dye works great with natural fibers and makes an especially effective natural camouflage. The only real drawback is how effective it is at staining. If you choose not to wear gloves, you risk a very long-term recoloring of your hands, and you should keep it away from your good clothes.

Black Walnut Dye
Materials:

- 10–15 black walnuts (This will make approximately 1 gallon of dye.)
- Water
- 1 tablespoon washing soda
- ½ teaspoon detergent

Procedure:

- Remove the walnut husks.
- Crush the hulls into pea-sized pieces.
- Using a nonreactive pot (stainless steel or enamelware—NOT aluminum), boil 1 gallon of water to a full boil.
- Add the crushed hulls and stir.
- Reduce heat and simmer, uncovered, for about an hour.
- While the dye is simmering, scour the material you plan to dye.
- To Scour:

- Using a nonreactive pot, add 1 tablespoon of washing soda and ½ teaspoon of detergent per 1 gallon of water and stir to dissolve.
- Boil water.
- Add the material you plan to dye and stir it into the water until it is fully saturated.
- Reduce heat and simmer uncovered for 1 hour.
- Rinse your materials to remove all the soap.
- Wring out the excess water.
- Add the damp, scoured material to the simmering dye bath.
- Continue to simmer, stirring occasionally, until the material is at least one shade darker than your desired color.
- Remove the material and rinse thoroughly until the water runs clear.
- Cool the dye bath and store in a glass container for reuse (do not pour out in your lawn as walnuts produce a natural herbicide).
- Allow your materials to dry completely before using. The color will lighten some as it dries and the dye oxidizes.

Note: Dyed clothing should be washed separately the first time. Excess dye will stain other clothes. After the initial wash, you may launder as usual with like-colored items.

Don't compost the hulls because they can suppress the growing of other plants. Tomatoes and apples, for example, won't grow near walnuts.

White Pine

White pine

White pine needle

Scientific Name: *Pinus strobus*

Type of Plant: Tree

Description: The white pine is a large, straight-stemmed tree with a pyramidal crown. It grows 50 to 100 feet tall. Pine leaves are two to five inches long, needle-shaped, and held in bundles of five (sometimes less). The needles are green with a blue tinge, flexible, and finely serrated. The leaf bundles live for eighteen months before they are shed and replaced by a new needle bundle. The seeds are less than one-fifth of an inch long and have a small wing that allows the seed to be wing dispersed. These seeds are held together in pinecones that are slender and three to six inches long and one and a half to two inches wide.

Natural Range: White pine naturally grows south from Canada to northern Georgia and northeastern Alabama and west to Minnesota. It prefers limestone soil with good drainage and mild summers. It has commercial use as lumber, so it may be planted outside its normal habitat.

Food Usage: Pine trees have many edible parts. The young needle shoots can be eaten, and the bark can be boiled and ground to use as a famine-food replacement for flour; but the most useful edible use of pine is to boil the needles for a tea that is high in vitamin A and C. Pine needle tea contains four to five times the vitamin C of fresh-squeezed orange juice and is high in vitamin A. It is also an expectorant and decongestant and can be used as an antiseptic wash.

Pine Needle Tea

Ingredients:
- Small handful of young needles
- Water

Procedure:
- Remove any of the brown, papery sheaths that may remain at the base of the needles.
- Chop the needles into small ¼ to ½ inch long pieces.
- Heat about a cup of water to just before boiling.
- Bring water almost to a boil.
- Pour the hot water over about a tablespoon of the chopped needles.
- Cover and allow to steep for 5–10 minutes.

Alternative Usage: Pine secretes a resin that closes cuts or broken limbs. This sticky sap has several uses for preppers or others during survival situations. As pine sap is exposed to air it will harden, but heating can soften it. The pine resin is waterproof, so it can be heated and applied to materials to seal seams. It is flammable and can be used to help start fires. Fatwood, which survivalists prize as a fire starter, is simply aged pine stumps that have the resin concentrated in the wood. The resin is sticky and can be used as glue.

Pine Pitch Glue

Materials:

- Pine pitch
- Charcoal
- Stick with a blunt end

Procedure:

- Warm the resin to liquid form (a double boiler is best used as pine pitch is very flammable).
- Crumble charcoal as fine as possible.
- Once the resin is liquid, remove it from the heat.
- Stir in powdered charcoal. Use one-third the amount of the charcoal as compared to the amount of liquid pine sap.
- Dip the stick in the liquid pine/charcoal mix. Do this repeatedly to form a large clump of pitch on the end of the stick. Once the glue hardens, the stick is easily stored for use.

To Use: Heat until pliable and rub over material to be joined.

Additionally, the pitch on the end of the stick may be lighted and used as a torch.

Note: Pine tar mixed with sulfur is useful to treat dandruff. Pine sap can be chewed like gum to clean your teeth. Pine tar can also be processed to make turpentine.

Willow

Willow

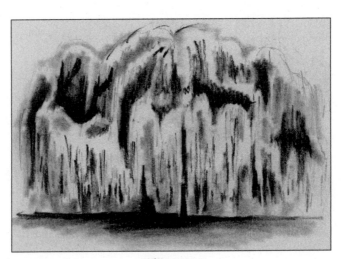

Willow tree

Scientific Name: *Salix babylonica*

Type of Plant: Tree

Description: Willows grow between 35 and 50 feet tall and develop a crown of the same size but have an extremely developed root system that is often larger than the tree. Willow roots have been known to destroy septic systems and sidewalks in developed areas. The wood is soft, usually pliant, and tough. The slender branches are filled with a watery bark sap that is heavily concentrated with salicylic acid.

The leaves are typically elongated, simple, and feather-veined.

Natural Range: Willows can be found throughout the United States, with weeping willows found primarily on the coasts. Because of its ability to absorb large amounts of water, they are often planted in flood zones or areas that need to be drained. The strong root system also prevents erosion.

Food Usage: Willow is edible, but it is unappetizing and is best considered to be a famine food. The inner bark is edible but first needs to be boiled several times to remove the bitterness caused by the salicylic acid. In Scandinavia, the boiled inner bark is dried, pulverized into dust, and added to flour to extend it. Historically, sawdust of all types has been used during famines as a flour extender. In my opinion, the best use of a willow tree from an edible perspective is to utilize willow saplings to make frog gigs. Since the edible parts of the tree are so bitter and it grows next to water, it makes sense to skip the bark and go for the meat.

Willow Sapling Frog Gig

Materials:

- Straight 6–8 foot willow sapling about 2 inches in diameter
- 3-inch long green twig about the size, of your little finger
- Cordage

Procedure:

- Trim the sapling of all limbs.
- Strip the bark off the smaller end of the stick, clearing a spot about 1 foot long.
- Place the root end of the sapling (the larger of the two ends) on a large rock or stump.
- Use a knife to split the thin end of the shaft 7 or 8 inches deep.
- Turn the sapling 90 degrees and make a second split to the same depth perpendicular to the first, making 4 equal pieces.
- Split the 3-inch twig into 2 halves.
- Wedge the first half into a split in the shaft to use as a spreader.
- Install the other spreader into the opposite split.
- Sharpen the 4 spread tines to turn them into sharpened points. You may add barbs, but the tines are spread enough so that barbs are both unnecessary and weakening of the points.

- Lash the spreaders to the shaft.
- Trim the spreaders flush with the lashings.

Keep in mind that when using the gig, light is refracted, making the object of attention look behind where it actually is, so aim low.

Alternative Usage: While the willow is not the greatest wild edible, I decided to include it because of its outstanding alternative uses, of which I am going to share two. Willow trees make an excellent rooting hormone that allows almost any cutting to be rooted. Willow roots so easily that the new growth can root itself similar to strawberries or blackberries. My dad recently cut some willow and the cut logs sent up shoots to root.

The second alternative use is extracting the salicylic acid, which is the natural version of aspirin. However, you should know that salicylic acid is rough on your stomach, which means you should not take more than a cup or two of willow tea without both understanding your body and seeking the advice of your doctor.

Willow Rooting Hormone

Materials:

- Water
- First year willow twigs with green or yellow bark

Procedure:

- Cut the twigs into 1-inch pieces.
- Place the chopped willow twigs in a container.
- Cover the twigs with boiling water.
- Let steep overnight.
- Separate the liquid from the twigs by carefully pouring the liquid through a strainer.
- To use, pour some willow water into a small jar, and place cuttings in the jar as you would put flowers in a vase.
- Let soak overnight.
- Remove from water and plant as you would any cutting.

You can keep the liquid for up to two months if you put it in a sealed jar in the refrigerator.

Willow Bark Aspirin

Materials:

- Willow tree
- Water

Procedure:

- Cut a square that is a little larger than an index card into the trunk of a willow tree. Ensure that this square is cut all the way through the bark, as you want to harvest the inner bark layer.
- Gently pry the square out, slowly going around the edges of your square to keep it as whole as possible. The goal is to get as much of the pink-tinged inner bark as possible.
- This scar will heal rather quickly, but it is best to harvest from a stand of trees and not focus on a single tree. If you cut out a ring all the way around the tree you will destroy its circulatory system and it will die.
- Scrape out the inner bark and collect at least 2 teaspoons of the bark.
- Boil water.
- Mix one cup of boiling water with 2 teaspoons of the inner bark and boil for 20 minutes.
- The tea will slowly take on a reddish brown color.
- Let steep 10 minutes.
- Filter out the solid bark. I use a very fine metal coffee filter, but in a pinch you can use a coffee filter over a glass or a cup with tiny holes poked into it.

This tea is good for minor pains, headaches, and anything aspirin would generally work for. If you are allergic to aspirin or are sensitive to it, then do not use this willow formula.

Do not drink more than four glasses a day.

Note: Hippocrates referred to the use of salicylic tea to reduce fevers around 400 BC. The use of natural salicylates for pain relief was widely used, and it was not until 1897 that the Bayer chemical company began producing a non-willow-based aspirin.

Suggested Reading

I really like the Peterson Field Guides, as well as the Audubon Society guides. I find that identification guides with full-color photographs are highly valuable for identification, with books on edibility and usage better for learning what to do with the plants identified.

- Peterson Field Guides
- *A Field Guide to Edible Wild Plants: Eastern and Central North America* by Lee Allen Peterson
- *Peterson Field Guide to Medicinal Plants and Herbs of Eastern and Central North America, Third Edition* by Steven Foster and James A. Duke
- *Plant Identification Terminology: An Illustrated Glossary* by James G. Harris and Melinda Woolf Harris
- *The American Horticultural Society Encyclopedia of Plants and Flowers* (American Horticultural Society Practical Guides) by Christopher Brickell
- *Trees of North America: A Guide to Field Identification* by C. Frank Brockman
- *Audubon Society Field Guide to North American Trees: Eastern Region* by National Audubon Society
- *The Forager's Harvest: A Guide to Identifying, Harvesting, and Preparing Edible Wild Plants* by Samuel Thayer
- *The North American Guide to Common Poisonous Plants and Mushrooms* by Nancy J. Turner and Patrick von Aderkas
- *Rosemary Gladstar's Medicinal Herbs: A Beginner's Guide* by Rosemary Gladstar
- *Nature's Garden: A Guide to Identifying, Harvesting, and Preparing Edible Wild Plants* by Samuel Thayer

- *Tom Brown's Guide to Wild Edible and Medicinal Plants* (Field Guide) by Tom Brown Jr.
- *The Illustrated Guide to Edible Wild Plants* by US Department of the Army
- *Edible Wild Plants: A North American Field Guide to Over 200 Natural Foods* by Thomas Elias and Peter Dykeman
- *The Herbal Medicine-Maker's Handbook: A Home Manual* by James Green

About the Author

David Nash is a dedicated prepper who uses self-reliance and disaster resilience in every portion of his life. Tired of having to wade through Internet misinformation to find out methods that work, he began documenting his journey to learn what does and does not work as he helps his family become better prepared for life's challenges.

This work involves a popular YouTube channel, website, and non-fiction books dedicated to DIY solutions for prepper problems.

You can find David online at www.tngun.com.

Other Skyhorse Publishing works by David Nash:

- *52 Prepper Projects*
- *52 Unique Techniques for Stocking Food for Preppers*
- *52 Prepper's Projects for Parents and Kids*

About the Illustrator

Sarah E. Cole has been an artist for more than twenty-five years. She sold her first painting before she was old enough to drive and quickly became someone who was sought out to paint on consignment. Sarah has painted everything from women's shelters to private homes, all before the age of eighteen.

As a teenager, she traveled to Matamoras, Mexico, on a mission trip with her church and was given the opportunity to paint a baptistery. Sarah went on to gain a BA in English from the University of Southern Mississippi and has released a few books as an author in her own right.

She is currently a resident of Neshoba County, Mississippi, where she raises her daughter.